ROSE
THEATRE
Kingston

William Shakespeare

LOVE'S LABOUR'S LOST

ROSE THEATRE
Kingston

Welcome to the Rose Theatre, Kingston, and to this performance of Shakespeare's *Love's Labour's Lost*.

This is a special moment in the Rose's history. Directed by our Emeritus Director, Sir Peter Hall, *Love's Labour's Lost* is the Rose's very first home-grown production. It has been made possible by a generous gift from the Rolex Institute.

Love's Labour's Lost was the first play Peter Hall ever directed at Stratford-upon-Avon and I'm thrilled that, fifty-two years later, he's chosen to launch the Rose's company with Shakespeare's great celebration of language. And we're delighted that he's assembled such a strong cast and creative team.

Love's Labour's Lost is the centrepiece of a festival of the spoken word. Other events at the Rose include children's workshops, public readings by local people of two of Shakespeare's early comedies (*The Two Gentlemen of Verona* and *The Comedy of Errors*), and one-off performances of *Venus and Adonis* and *The Rape of Lucrece*. This culminates in the Sunday Telegraph & Rose Theatre Poetry for Performance Competition, spearheaded by Andrew Motion, Poet Laureate.

The Rose is going from strength to strength. The autumn season has been a remarkable success and we are proud to be presenting our second in-house production at Christmas, a new stage adaptation of Charles Dickens' classic, *A Christmas Carol*. But with hardly any public funding we face grave financial challenges. Do please give what you can to make the Rose bloom.

I hope you enjoy this performance of Shakespeare's youthful comedy.

Stephen Unwin
Artistic Director

Love's Labour's Lost
has been made possible
by a generous gift from
the Rolex Institute.

THE
ROLEX INSTITUTE

Photograph by Chris Pearsall

ROSE THEATRE
Kingston

ABOUT THE ROSE THEATRE, KINGSTON

The Rose Theatre, Kingston opened in January 2008
to great acclaim, and has hosted many successful visits.
Love's Labour's Lost is the Rose's first home-grown production.

**"The theatre, which has been doggedly championed by Sir
Peter Hall, is a palpable hit"** Telegraph

The auditorium of the Rose takes its inspiration from the original
Elizabethan theatre on London's bankside, in which some of
Shakespeare's plays premiered. The great circle at the heart of
the Rose's ground plan provides the template for everything it
does: all-embracing, accessible, warm-hearted, popular, serious,
intelligent and stylish. The Rose aims to be a centre of excellence
and a place of learning.

Productions of scenic simplicity and human scale embrace the
particular features of the Rose's exceptional stage and auditorium,
and are characterised by an uncompromising emphasis on the
centrality of language and the spoken word in all its forms.

Life President	*David Jacobs CBE DL*
Director Emeritus	*Sir Peter Hall*
Artistic Director	*Stephen Unwin*
Executive Director	*David Fletcher*
General Manager	*Jerry Gunn*
Director of Marketing & Communications	*Lucy Goldsborough*
Development Director	*Matthew Cull*

www.rosetheatrekingston.org

CAST

THE KING OF NAVARRE	Dan Fredenburgh
LONGAVILLE)	Nicholas Bishop
DUMAINE) his lords	Nick Barber
BEROWNE)	Finbar Lynch
DULL, a constable	Peter Gordon
COSTARD, a countryman	Greg Haiste
DON ADRIANO DE ARMADO, a Spanish braggart	Peter Bowles
MOTH, his page	Kevin Trainor
JAQUENETTA, a dairymaid	Ella Smith
THE PRINCESS OF FRANCE	Rachel Pickup
BOYET, her chamberlain	Michael Mears
MARIA)	Nelly Harker
KATHERINE) her ladies	Sally Scott
ROSALINE)	Susie Trayling
HOLOFERNES, a pedantic schoolmaster	William Chubb
SIR NATHANIEL, a curate)	
FORESTER)	Paul Bentall
MERCADÉ, a royal messenger)	

CREATIVE TEAM

Director	Peter Hall
Associate Director	Cordelia Monsey
Set & Costume Designer	Christopher Woods
Lighting Designer	James Whiteside
Music	Mick Sands
Sound Designer	Gregory Clarke
Costume Supervisor	Joan Hughes
Movement	Jackie Snow (née Matthews)
Casting	Gemma Hancock & Sam Stevenson

PRODUCTION TEAM

Production Manager	Wayne Parry
Company Stage Manager	Lisa Hall
Deputy Stage Manager	Holly Haydn
Assistant Stage Manager	Lucy Porter
Wardrobe Manager	Michelle Tilling
Schools Workshops	Danielle Coleman

PRODUCTION ACKNOWLEDGEMENTS

Playtext & Programme Notes	Roger Warren
Costumes Supplied by	Angels Costumiers
Wigs	Brian Peters of Angels Costumiers
Set built by	Set-up Scenery Ltd
Production Photographer	Nobby Clark
Print Design	Sarah Hyndman for With Relish
Audio Description	William Clancy

CAST:

NICK BARBER
Dumaine

Theatre: *I Saw Myself* (The Wrestling School), *Othello* (Shakespeare's Globe), *Our Country's Good* (Liverpool Everyman), *Faust* (Punch Drunk), *The Canterbury Tales* (RSC), *An Inspector Calls* (National Tour), *The Gentlemen from Olmedo*, *The Venetian Twins* (Watermill Theatre), *Julius Caesar* (Menier Chocolate Factory), *Romeo and Juliet* (Southwark Playhouse).

Film: *Colour Me Kubrick, Stage Beauty*.

Television: *Robinson Crusoe, Bitter & Twisted, The Waltz King, The Brief, Midsomer Murders*.

PAUL BENTALL
Sir Nathaniel / Forester / Mercadé

Theatre includes**:** *The Burial at Thebes* (Nottingham Playhouse, Barbican, USA Tour & Rose Theatre, Kingston), *Habeas Corpus, Measure for Measure* (Theatre Royal Bath & National Tour), *You Never Can Tell* (Garrick Theatre), *The Mikado* (Orange Tree Theatre, Richmond), *Brighton Rock* (Almeida Theatre), *The Coffee House* (Chichester Festival Theatre), *Uncle Vanya* (Sheffield Crucible), *The Man Who Had All the Luck* (Young Vic), *Darwin's Flood* (Bush Theatre), *Salome and the Trial* (World Tour). For the RSC: *Eastward Ho!, Edward III, Love in a Wood, Jubilee, A Servant of Two Masters, Cymbeline, The Spanish Tragedy, Henry VIII, Richard III, Faust (The Poet), Julius Caesar, The Taming of the Shrew, Wildest Dreams, Showboat*. For the National Theatre: *Theatre of Blood, The Trial (The Bailiff), A Month in the Country, Sergeant Musgrave's Dance, Danton's Death, Much Ado About Nothing, Caritas Christi, The Prince of Homburg, Don Juan, Lorenzaccio, You Can't Take It With You, Strider Story of a Horse, The Ancient Mariner, Jackobowski and the Colonel*.

Television: *Wolfenden, Silent Witness, Pie in the Sky, Why We Went to War, The Governor, A Dark Adapted Eye, Between the Lines, The New Statesman, Spender, Casualty, French Fields, As You Like It*.

Film: *Vanity Fair, Blackball, First Knight*.

NICHOLAS BISHOP
Longaville

Theatre: *A Midsummer Night's Dream* (OUDS), *One Flew Over the Cuckoo's Nest, A Streetcar Named Desire, The Oxford Revue*, (Oxford Playhouse), *Romeo and Juliet, Design for Living, Twelfth Night* (Old Fire Station, Oxford), *Skylight* (O'Reilly Theatre, Oxford) *Oleanna, Sexual Perversity in Chicago, Jail Talk* (Burton Taylor Theatre, Oxford*), The Merchant of Venice, The Rivals, Hamlet, Macbeth, After Magritte* (Ryan Theatre, Harrow), *A Triple Bill of Shame* (Greyfriar's Kirkhouse, Edinburgh Festival Fringe 2004).

Television: *Hustle*.

PETER BOWLES
Don Adriano de Armado

Theatre includes leading roles in: *The Happy Haven* (Royal Court), *Platonov* with Rex Harrison (Royal Court), *JB* with Sir Donald Sinden, and *Bonne Soupe* with Carol Browne (Phoenix & Wyndham's Theatres). West End productions for Peter Hall include Molière's *The School for Wives* and *The Misanthrope*, Shaw's *Major Barbara* (all Piccadilly Theatre) Rattigan's *Separate Tables*, and at Theatre Royal Haymarket, Kaufman's *The Royal Family* and Noel Coward's *Hay Fever*, both with Dame Judi Dench. Other theatre credits include *Dirty Linen, The Afternoon Men* (both Arts Theatre), *Look After Lulu* (Theatre Royal Haymarket) *Present Laughter* (Wyndham's Theatre), *Born in the Gardens* (Globe Theatre), Archie Rice in *The Entertainer* (Shaftesbury Theatre), Ayckbourn's *Man of the Moment* with Sir Michael Gambon (Globe Theatre) & *Absent Friends* (Garrick Theatre), *In Praise of Love* (Apollo Theatre), *Gangster No 1* (Almeida Theatre), *The Beau* (Theatre Royal Haymarket), *Hedda Gabler* (National Tour), *Our Song* (National Tour), *Sleuth* (Apollo Theatre, London), *Wait Until Dark* (Garrick Theatre), as Terence Rattigan in *Joe and I* (Kings Head), *The Old Masters (Comedy Theatre)*, and *The Waltz of the Toreadors* (Chichester Festival Theatre). In 2008, Peter toured in a production of Ayckbourn's *Relatively Speaking*.

Film includes: *The Yellow Rolls Royce, Endless Night, Blow Up, Laughter in the Dark, The Offence, The Legend of Hell House, The Charge of the Light Brigade, A Day in the Death of Joe Egg, The Hollywood Ten, Colour Me Kubrick, Freebird* and *The Bank Job*. Peter was also the driving force and Executive Producer of *Gangster No 1*.

Television series include; *Tales of the Unexpected – Neck; Rumpole of the Bailey, To the Manor Born, Only When I Laugh, The Bounder, Executive Stress, Vice Versa, The Irish RM, Lytton's Diary* (also devised), *Perfect Scoundrels* (also co-devised). Television films include: *Shadow on the Sun, Shelley and Byron, Isadora Duncan, Love and War, Ballet Shoes* and *Poirot*. Peter also produced and starred in *Running Late* (winning Golden Gate Film Award at San Francisco Film festival).

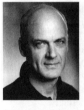

WILLIAM CHUBB
Holofernes

Theatre includes: *The Sea, Hay Fever* (Theatre Royal Haymarket), *The History Boys* (National Tour), *Galileo's Daughter, Don Juan, Man and Superman, Design for Living, Fight for Barbara* (Theatre Royal Bath), *You Never Can Tell* (Theatre Royal Bath, Garrick Theatre London & Tour), *Whose Life is it Anyway?* (Comedy Theatre*), Justifying War: Scenes from The Hutton Enquiry* (Tricycle Theatre), *Iphigenia* (Rehearsed Reading – Lyric Hammersmith), *Homebody Kabul* (Young Vic), *A Raisin in the Sun* (Young Vic & Salisbury Playhouse), *Ghosts* (English Touring Theatre National Tour), *He Stumbled* (National Tour), *Burning Issues* (Hampstead Theatre), *Judith* (Wrestling School & National Tour), *Tulip Futures* (Soho Theatre) *The School Mistress* (Chichester Festival Theatre) *Time and the Conways* (Old Vic). For the National Theatre: *The*

London Cuckolds, The Invention of Love, The Princes Play, The Madness of King George III (also New York), *Trelawney of the Wells*. For the RSC: *Conversation, The Silent Woman, Three Sisters, The New Inn, The Taming of the Shrew, Julius Caesar, The Merchant of Venice*. For Cheek by Jowl at the RSC: *The Man of Mode, A Midsummer Night's Dream*.

Film includes: *Gladiatress, Mrs Caldicot's Cabbage War, The Affair of the Necklace, Milk, The Woodlanders*.

Television includes: *The Bill, Holby City, Phoo Action, The Montagu Trial, Casanova's Lost Love Letters, Absolute Power, Cherished, Trial and Retribution, Midsomer Murders, Murder in Mind, Heartbeat, A & E III, Relic Hunter, Active Defence, Playing the Field, Randall & Hopkirk Deceased, Extremely Dangerous, Rocket to the Moon, The Ambassador (Series 1 & 2), Breakout, Kavanagh QC, To Play the King, House of Cards, The Buddha of Suburbia, Sleepers, Signs and Wonders, Just Us, Poirot* and numerous commercials.

Radio: *The Invention of Love, The Pimlico Poisoner, Twelfth Night*.

DAN FREDENBURGH
King of Navarre

Theatre: *The Portrait of a Lady* (Peter Hall Company at Theatre Royal Bath, Tour & Rose Theatre, Kingston), *A Few Good Men* (Theatre Royal Haymarket), *Children of a Lesser God* (Salisbury Playhouse), *Sunday Father* (Hampstead Theatre), *Mnemoic* (Complicite Theatre Company International Tour), *An Inspector Calls* (Garrick Theatre, London), *Out in the Cold, Le Chandelier* (Greenwich Studio),

A Woman's Comedy (Wimbledon Theatre), *Skinwalker* (BAC), *Barefoot in the Park* (Frinton Rep).

Film: *The Bourne Ultimatum, Earthquakes* (short film), *There For Me, Land of the Blind, Love Actually, Al's Lads, Café de Paris, Brothers, The Lake District, The Sweet Rain*.

Television: *Ashes to Ashes, Silent Witness, Waking the Dead, Donovan, The Bill, Holby City, Doctors, Lexx, Bad Girls, Queen of Swords, Sword of Honour, The Knock, Douch Anglais*.

PETER GORDON
Dull

Theatre: *Oedipus Trilogy, Anthony & Cleopatra, Entertaining Strangers, Coriolanus* (all directed by Peter Hall), *Wild Honey, The American Clock, State of Revolution, the late Shakespeares* (National Theatre), *The Way of the World* (Young Vic), *The School for Scandal* (Chichester Festival Theatre), *Marya* (Old Vic), *Born Yesterday, Elektra, Caste* (Greenwich Theatre), *Noises Off* (Piccadilly Theatre), *The Tempest* . Provincial Theatre credits include leading roles in: *Dr Faustus, An Inspector Calls, The Caretaker, Twelfth Night, The Birthday Party, All My Sons*. In productions directed by Peter Hall: *Twelfth Night, Tartuffe, An Ideal Husband, She Stoops to Conquer, Hamlet, Amadeus* and *Lady Windermere's Fan*. In productions directed by Peter Hall at the Old Vic: *Waste, King Lear, The Seagull, As You Like It* (also Theatre Royal Bath, US & UK Tours). In productions directed by Peter Hall at Theatre Royal Bath: *Galileo's Daughter, Don Juan, Much Ado About Nothing*.

Film: *A Bridge Too Far, Blue Ice, Bridget Jones, The Edge of Reason, Sparkle.*

Television: *Brideshead Revisited, Scum, Oranges Are Not The Only Fruit, The Bill, London's Burning, The Camomile Lawn, Peak Practice, Dangerfield, Inspector Morse, The Last Detective, Murder in Mind, Rosemary & Thyme, Margaret, Doctors.*

GREG HAISTE
Costard

Theatre: *Black Comedy, The Bowmans* (Watermill Theatre, Newbury), *The Play What I Wrote* (National Tour), *Henry IV* (Orange Tree Theatre, Richmond), *All in the Timing* (Peepolykus), *The Madness of George III* (Birmingham Repertory Theatre & West Yorkshire Playhouse), *The Accrington Pals, Hamlet, Rosencrantz and Guildenstern are Dead, The Lady in the Van* (West Yorkshire Playhouse), *A Midsummer Night's Dream* (English Shakespeare Company), *The Tempest* (Southwark Playhouse), *Macbeth, Measure for Measure* (Theatre Unlimited), *Away, Europe* (Traverse Theatre, Edinburgh), *Services* (Gate Theatre), *Romeo and Juliet* (Young Shakespeare Company), *It Runs in the Family* (E&B National A Tour), *Lulu, RUR, The Railway Children* (Harrogate Theatre), *Teechers* (Really Youthful Company)

Film: *To Curry Favour*

Television: *Touch Me I'm Karen Taylor, Emmerdale, Jane Hall, Heartbeat, True Crimes, See How They Run.*

NELLY HARKER
Maria

Theatre: *The Portrait of a Lady* (Peter Hall Company at Theatre Royal Bath & Rose Theatre, Kingston), *The Heiress* (The Mill at Sonning), *The Importance of Being Earnest* (Chichester Festival Theatre Gala), *Gaslight, Table Manners, Chapter Two, The Public Eye, Blithe Spirit, The Diaries of Adam and Eve* (Frinton Rep Theatre), *The Tempest* (Cliveden Open Air Theatre), *Helen of Troy, The Front Page* (Webber Douglas Academy).

FINBAR LYNCH
Berowne

Theatre includes: For the Peter Hall Company: Gilbert Osmond in *The Portrait of a Lady,* Torvald Helmer in *A Doll's House* (Theatre Royal Bath & Rose Theatre, Kingston). For the RSC: Proteus in *Two Gentlemen of Verona,* Surly in *The Alchemist,* Bruce in *The Virtuoso,* Wendoll in *A Woman Killed With Kindness,* Mark Antony in *Julius Caesar,* Zak in *Amphibians,* Lucio in *Measure for Measure,* Aufidius in *Coriolanus,* Alonso in *The Tempest,* Puck in *A Midsummer Night's Dream* (also Lunt-Fontanne Theatre, Broadway), Cassius in *Julius Caesar.* For the National Theatre: Edmond in *King Lear,* Enobarbus in *Antony and Cleopatra,* Canary Jim in *Not About Nightingales* (also Circle In The Square Theatre, Broadway, Best actor Nomination Drama Desk Awards, Best Supporting Actor nomination Tony awards) Gibbs in *The Hothouse.* For the Donmar Warehouse: Manus in *Translations*, Eddie in *Fool For Love*, Venus in *To The Green Fields Beyond*, Polymestor in *Hecuba*. Theatre credits in Dublin include: Peer in *Peer Gynt* (Best Actor, Irish Theatre Awards), Sydney in *Absurd Person Singular*, Jack Absolute in *The Rivals*, Charles Surface in *The School for Scandal*, Bazarov in *Fathers and Sons* (all Gate Theatre), Christy Mahon in *The Playboy of the Western World* (Abbey Theatre), Gar Public in *Philadelphia Here I Come*, Mark in *Mass Appeal* (Gaiety Theatre) Paddy Maguire in *Goodbye to the Hill*, Gary Lejuene in *Noises Off* (Olympia Theatre). Other theatre includes: McCann in *The Birthday Party* (Duchess Theatre), Boffi in *As You Desire Me* (Playhouse Theatre, London), Vince in *Three Sisters on Hope Street* (Hampstead Theatre & Liverpool Everyman Theatre), Jesus in *Messiah* (Riverside Studios), Pastor Manders in *Ghosts* (Gate Theatre), Tuzenbach in *Three Sisters* (Royal Court & Gate Theatre, Dublin), Jean in *Miss Julie* (Greenwich Theatre), Iago in *Othello* (Greenwich Theatre & Royal & Derngate Theatres, Northampton), Macbeth in *Macbeth* (Crucible Theatre, Sheffield), James Tyrone in *A Moon for the Misbegotten* (Royal Exchange, Manchester).

Film: *Matilde, To Kill A King, Lost Battalion, King Lear, The Scolds Bridle, A Midsummer Night's Dream, The Schooner, The Wild Ponies. Mind Games, The Scar, A Secret Audience, King Lear, Rawhead Rex.*

Television: *George Gently, The Eejits, Proof* (Series 1 & 2), *Dalziel & Pascoe, Waking the Dead, Holby City* (BBC), *Expensive Silence* (Proof), *Red Cap, Atilla The Hun, Second Sight, Mind Games, Small World, Between The Lines, Glenroe* (Series 1-5), *Riddlers Moon, Three Wishes for Jamie, Miller Shorts.*

MICHAEL MEARS
Boyet

Theatre: *Measure for Measure* (Peter Hall Company & RSC), *You Never Can Tell* (Peter Hall Company at Garrick Theatre, London), *Harper Regan* (National Theatre), *The Tempest, Kind Hearts & Coronets* (Queens Theatre, Hornchurch), *Someone Who'll Watch Over Me* (Manchester Library Theatre), *Osama The Hero* (Hampstead Theatre), *Twelfth Night, The Hypochondriac* (Octagon Theatre, Bolton), *Jubilee* (RSC), *Saint Joan* (Birmingham Repertory Theatre), *The Goodbye Girl* (Albery Theatre), *The Odd Couple* (York Theatre Royal), *Conversations with my Father* (Old Vic), *Oliver!* (Belgrade Theatre, Coventry).

Film: *Invisible Eyes, The Oxford Murders, Sylvia, Four Weddings & A Funeral, Queen of Hearts, Little Dorrit.*

Television: *The Colour of Magic, Sold, Sharpe's Rifles* (3 series), *Marie Lloyd, According to Bex, My Family* (Christmas Special), *The Lenny Henry Show - Delbert Wilkins* (2 series), *The Bill, Mary and Jesus, The Seventh Scroll, The Old Curiosity Shop.*

Writing: *Tomorrow We Do The Sky, Soup* (Traverse Theatre, Edinburgh and Lyric Studio, Hammersmith, and on BBC Radio 4. Winner of Fringe First award), *A Slight Tilt To The Left, Slow Train To Woking, Uncle Happy, Jam and Arnold Darwin's Getting Better* (solo plays commissioned for BBC Radio 4.)

RACHEL PICKUP
Princess of France

Theatre: *The 39 Steps* (Criterion Theatre), *Troilus and Cressida* (Edinburgh International Festival & Royal Shakespeare Theatre Stratford), *A Midsummer Night's Dream* (RSC & London Sinfonia), *Two Gentlemen of Verona* (RSC), *Julius Caesar* (RSC & Lyric Hammersmith), *Paradox* (RSC The Other Place), *Dr Foster* (Menier Chocolate Factory), *Hamlet* (Birmingham Repertory Theatre & Royal Lyceum Theatre Edinburgh), *King Lear* (English Touring Theatre National Tour & Old Vic), *Time and the Conways, The Fall Guy* (Manchester Royal Exchange), *The Sea* (Chichester Festival Theatre), *Barefoot in the Park* (Jermyn Street Theatre), *Twelfth Night* (Theatr Clwyd), *Three Sisters, Home Truths* (Birmingham Repertory Theatre), *All's Well That Ends Well* (Oxford Stage Company National Tour), *Fortune's Fool* (Chichester Festival Theatre & Tour), *Way Upstream* (Sheffield Crucible).

Film: *AKA, ESN* (short film), *Basil.*

Television: *Midsomer Murders, Doctors, Rosemary & Thyme, Holby City, Jeffrey Archer – The Truth, Relic Hunters, Victoria & Albert, No Bananas, Soldier, Soldier.*

SALLY SCOTT
Katherine

Theatre: *Boeing Boeing* (Comedy Theatre), *Sweet Bird of Youth* (Rehearsed Reading – Garrick Theatre), *Who's Afraid of Virginia Woolf, Fool for Love* (Apollo Theatre), *Coward* (Soho Theatre), *Serenading Louie* (RADA). Whilst training: *An Ideal Husband, Arcadia, Dancing at Lughnasa, Guys & Dolls, All My Sons.*

Film: *Things To See, Adjustment.*

ELLA SMITH
Jaquenetta

Theatre: *Fat Pig* (Trafalgar Studios & Comedy Theatre), *The Pocket Orchestra* (Trafalgar Studios), *Hyde Park, The Jews* (Rehearsed Readings at Shakespeare's Globe), *William Poel Festival* (Shakespeare's Globe). For National Youth Theatre: *The Threepenny Opera, Nicholas Nickleby* (Lyric Theatre Hammersmith),

Television: *Sold, Strictly Confidential* (ITV), *Cape Wrath, Meadowlands* (Channel 4), *Holby City* (BBC).

Radio: *Scandinavian Dreams, The Sea, The Man Who Built Tunnels, Jane's Story, The Fossilist* (all BBC).

KEVIN TRAINOR
Moth

Theatre: *2000 Feet Away* (Bush Theatre), *Bent* (Trafalgar Studios), *Gladiator Games* (Theatre Royal Stratford East), *Twelfth Night, Solstice, The Comedy of Errors, Eric La Rue* (RSC – 2005 Season), *Fishbowl* (Latchmere Theatre).

Film: *Hellboy, The Hole, Pies Day.*

Television: *John Adams* (HBO), *The Catherine Tate Show* (BBC), *Titanic: Birth of a Legend* (Granada), *Tripping Over, The Commander.*

Radio: *The Hiring Fair* (BBC Radio Ulster).

SUSIE TRAYLING
Rosaline

Theatre includes: For the Peter Hall Company: *The Portrait of a Lady, A Doll's House* (Theatre Royal Bath & Rose Theatre, Kingston), *Measure for Measure, Habeus Corpus.* For the National Theatre: *Women of Troy, Dream Play, Iphigenia at Aulis, The Forest.* Other credits include: *Closer, The Importance of Being Earnest* (Theatre Royal, Northampton), *Don't Look Now* (Sheffield Lyceum & Lyric Hammersmith), *Skylight* (Stephen Joseph Theatre, Scarborough), *Twelfth Night* (West Yorkshire Playhouse), *Waters of the Moon* (Salisbury Playhouse), *The Mob* (Orange Tree Theatre, Richmond), *Anna Karenina* (Nominated – Best Actress, Manchester Evening News Awards), *Private Lives* (Bolton Octagon Theatre), *Camera Obscura* (Almeida), *Hamlet* (Northcott Theatre, Exeter), *Edward II* (Sheffield Crucible), *Kiss of Death* (Mill at Sonning), *Private View* (Regent's Park Theatre).

Film includes: *Fragile, Piccadilly Jim, Fog Bound, All the Queen's Men*

Television includes: *The Bill, Casualty, Heartbeat, Inspector Lynley Mysteries, Hearts and Bones, Holby City.*

CREATIVE TEAM:

PETER HALL Director

Peter Hall was born in Bury St Edmunds and educated at the Perse School and St Catharine's College, Cambridge. After his professional directing debut in Windsor, he ran the Arts Theatre, London where productions included the premiere, in 1955, of the English language version of Beckett's *Waiting for Godot*. He was the Founder and Director of the Royal Shakespeare Company (1960-68); and was Director of the Royal National Theatre for fifteen years (1973-88) moving the company into the theatres on the South Bank. From 1984 to 1990 he was Artistic Director of Glyndebourne Festival Opera.

In 1988 he launched the Peter Hall Company with productions of *Orpheus Descending* (with Vanessa Redgrave) and *The Merchant of Venice* (with Dustin Hoffman) since when it has staged some sixty productions in association with a number of well-known producing partners. As well as a landmark season at the Old Vic in the mid 1990's, since 2003 the Peter Hall Company has given an annual, and highly successful, Summer Residency at the Theatre Royal in Bath. A large number of the Company's productions have been seen on extended UK tours, in the West End and also abroad in the US, Australia and in Europe.

The Peter Hall company celebrated its 20th anniversary this year with a sixth summer residency at the Theatre Royal where the season included Peter Hall's new productions of Ibsen's *A Doll's House*, Nicki Frei's adaptation of Henry James's *Portrait of a Lady* and Stephen Unwin's production of Peter Nichols' *Born in the Garden*.

These productions have also been seen at The Rose Theatre.

Other recent Peter Hall Company productions have included Harold Pinter's *Betrayal* (with Janie Dee, Aiden Gillet and Hugo Speer); *As You Like It* (with Rebecca Hall and Dan Stevens – which also presented at The Rose); *The Dresser* (with Nicholas Lyndhurst and Julian Glover); *Whose Life is it Anyway* (with Kim Cattrall); *You Never Can Tell* (with Edward Fox); the 50th Anniversary production of *Waiting for Godot; Hay Fever* (starring Judi Dench), *Amy's View* and *The Vortex* both with Felicity Kendal and *Pygmalion* with Tim Pigott-Smith and Michelle Dockery.

Peter Hall was appointed Director of The Rose in 2003 and became Director Emeritus earlier this year. *Love's Labour's Lost* is his fourth production to be seen at The Rose since the theatre opened in January with his acclaimed version of *Uncle Vanya.*

In addition to some twenty opera productions for Glyndebourne, Peter Hall has also directed for many of the world's major houses including the Royal Opera, the Metropolitan Opera, Bayreuth Festival Opera, Los Angeles Opera, the Lyric Opera of Chicago and Houston Grand Opera.

Peter Hall's films for cinema and TV include *Three Into Two Won't Go, Akenfield, The Homecoming, The Camomile Lawn* and *The Final Passage.* In 2005 he was the subject of a special South Bank Show – *Peter Hall, 50 Years in Theatre* – broadcast in honour of his 75th birthday. He is also the author of a number of books on and about the theatre including, most recently, *Shakespeare's Advice to the Players*, a detailed analysis of the art of verse speaking.

His many arts awards and nominations include two Tony Awards and three for Lifetime Achievement. He was knighted in 1977 for services to the Theatre. Peter Hall holds honorary doctorates from a number of Universities including Cambridge, York, Bath and London and is Chancellor of Kingston University.

CORDELIA MONSEY
Associate Director

Cordelia's most recent work includes the UK premiere of Athol Fugard's *Victory* at the Theatre Royal Bath as part of the 2007 Peter Hall Season.

Cordelia has worked as Associate Director to Peter Hall on seasons at Bath, The Old Vic, in the West End and on tour. Productions include: *Pygmalion* (Bath, 2007 and Old Vic, 2008), *Uncle Vanya* (English Touring Theatre National Tour, opening at Rose Theatre, Kingston), *Old Times* (Theatre Royal Bath & National Tour, *Waiting for Godot* (Theatre Royal Bath & West End), *The Bacchai* (National Theatre & Epidaurus)

Assistant Director credits include: *Amadeus* for Peter Hall (Old Vic), *We Happy Few* for Trevor Nunn (Gielgud Theatre), *Richard III, King Lear* (National Theatre & International Tour) *The Fairy Queen* (Aix-en-Provence Festival), *Macbeth, The Tempest, Restoration* and *Nicholas Nickleby* (RSC, London, New York and Los Angeles), *Carmen* (Glyndebourne).

Directing credits include: *Home, Private Lives* (NT Platforms*), Roman and Marys, Anna on Anna* (Offstage Downstage Theatre), *Speak of the Devil* (Edinburgh Festival), Ionesco's *Macbett* and Fielding's *Tom Thumb* (RSC & Almeida), *New Plays* (RSC Winter Festival), *Golden Girls* (Leeds Playhouse), *Romeo and Juliet* and *Deathtrap* (Hornchurch), *Betrayal* & *The Sport of My Mad Mother*

(Leatherhead), *Blithe Spirit, Village Wooing, Dial M for Murder, Ball Boys, Swan Song* and *Zoo Story* (Ipswich), *Ain't a Woman* (Riverside, Soho Poly and Edinburgh Festival).

CHRISTOPHER WOODS
Set & Costume Designer

Theatre includes: *The Portrait of a Lady, A Doll's House* (Theatre Royal Bath, Tour & Rose Theatre, Kingston), *Once Upon A Time at the Adelphi, Much Ado About Nothing, Billy Liar* (Everyman Theatre, Liverpool), *Pygmalion, Little Nell* (Theatre Royal Bath & Old Vic), *Charley's Aunt, An Hour & A Half Late* (Theatre Royal Bath*), A Right Royal Farce, Who's the Daddy* (Kings Head Theatre), *Daisy Miller* (Malvern Festival Theatre & UK Tour), *Patti Boulaye's Sundance* (Hackney Empire), *Beyond Reasonable Doubt* (Mercury Theatre, Colchester), *Never the Sinner* (Library Theatre Manchester), *The Chimes at Midnight* (Chichester Festival Theatre), *The Betrayal of Nora Blake* (Jermyn Street Theatre), *Les Enfants du Paradis* (RSC at the Barbican), *Good Morning Bill* (Palace Theatre Watford), *The Destiny of Me* (Leicester Haymarket Theatre).

West End credits include: *Never Forget* (Savoy Theatre & UK Tour), *Six Dance Lessons in Six Weeks* (Theatre Royal Haymarket), *Daddy Cool* (Shaftesbury Theatre) *Songs My Mother Taught Me* (Savoy), *Beautiful & Damned* (Lyric Shaftesbury Avenue), *Cooper! Jus' Like That* (Garrick Theatre & UK Tour), *The Mystery of Charles Dickens* (Albery & Comedy Theatres, & UK Tour), *Jesus My Boy* (Apollo Theatre), *H.R.H* (Playhouse Theatre), Pygmalion (Albery Theatre), *The Importance of Being Oscar* (Savoy Theatre), *Murder is Easy* (Duke of York's Theatre), *The Pyjama Game* (Victoria Palace

Theatre), *Shades* (Albery), *The Rat Pack – Live from Las Vegas* (Strand Theatre & European Tour).

International credits include *Daddy Cool* (Berlin), *The Mystery of Charles Dickens* (Broadway, Chicago Shakespeare Theatre and Australian Tour), *Chicago* (Kuala Lumpur), *Sweetbox* (Japanese and Korean Tours), *Celtic Tiger, Once Upon A Time* (Endemol, Denmark), *Copacabana* (Copenhagen), *Chess* (Rossen & Ronnow Musical Productions), *An Evening with Burt Bacharach* (Melbourne, Australia).

Concerts include: *The Stephen Oliver Trilogy* (Covent Garden Festival), *Desire* (Birmingham Contemporary Music Group), *Jerusalem for Reconciliation* (Royal Albert Hall), *Stevie Wants to Play the Blues* (Los Angeles Theatre Centre), *Poe – More Tales of Mystery and Imagination* (Abbey Road).

Opera includes: *Fierrabras, La Finta Semplice* (Buxton Festival), *The Magic Flute* (RNCM), *The Consul* (Opera Holland Park), *Il Turco in Italia, Il Tabarro, Suor Angelica, Gianni Schicci* (Broomhill Opera), *Madame Butterfly, La Traviata, Die Fledermaus, Don Pasquale* (Clonter Opera), *La Boheme* (British Youth Opera, Sadlers Wells).

Film: *A Christmas Carol* (Miramax), *The Ballad of the Sad Café,* (Merchant Ivory), *The Lake, Camilla & William, Soft Top Hard Shoulder, Bird of Prey, The Von Recklinhausen Story, The Miracle.*

Television: *An Evening with Charles Dickens, Charles Dickens at Christmas.*

JAMES WHITESIDE Lighting Designer

Theatre includes: *The Female of the Species* (Vaudeville Theatre), *Funny Girl* (Chichester Festival Theatre), *Never Forget* (Savoy Theatre & National Tour), *Salonika* (West Yorkshire Playhouse), *Animal Farm* (Peter Hall Company, Theatre Royal Bath), *Footloose* (West End and National Tour), *This Piece of Earth, The Early Bird* (Ransom Productions, Belfast), *Plunder, Copenhagen* (Watermill Theatre, Newbury), *Vanity Fair, Grimm Nights & Everafter Days, Alice's Adventures in Wonderland* (Chicken Shed Theatre), *Poor Mrs Pepys* (New Vic, Newcastle-under-Lyme), *Fen, Five Kinds of Silence* (Live Theatre, Newcastle), *Calamity Jane* (West End and National Tour), National Tours of *Donkey's Years, Heroes* and *Art.* For Tall Stories Theatre Company: *The Gruffalo* (West End and Off-Broadway), *Snow White* (Off-Broadway), *The Gruffalo's Child* (National Tour). As Assistant Lighting Designer: *Mary Stuart* (Apollo Theatre), *Guys and Dolls* (Piccadilly Theatre, National Tour and Australia), *Mary Poppins* (Prince Edward Theatre), *Desperately Seeking Susan* (Novello Theatre), *I Masnadieri* (Teatro Comunale, Bologna).

Opera includes: *Maria De Buenos Aires* (Theatre Royal Bath), *HMS Pinafore* (Carl Rosa Opera), *Madama Butterfly* (US Tour).

MICK SANDS Music

Theatre includes: *The Vortex* (Peter Hall Company, West End and Tour), *The Burial at Thebes* (Nottingham Playhouse, UK Tour, American Tour & Rose Theatre, Kingston), *Uncle Vanya* (English Touring Theatre National Tour, opening at Rose Theatre, Kingston), *Little Nell, Victory, Measure for Measure, Miss Julie, Habeas Corpus, Galileo's Daughter,*

Don Juan (Peter Hall Company), *Much Ado About Nothing, Private Lives* (Peter Hall Company at Theatre Royal Bath) *Prometheus Bound* (Sound Theatre, Leicester Square), *Believe What You Will, Hecuba, Beauty and the Beast, Eastward Ho!* (RSC), *Alcmeon in Corinth* (Live Theatre, Newcastle), *The Cherry Orchard, Three Sisters* (Oxford Stage Company), *Twelfth Night* (Southwark Playhouse), *Sive* (Druid Theatre, Galway & Irish Tour), *Tantalus* (Denver Theatre, Colorado & RSC Tour), *Beauty and the Beast* (Young Vic & International Festival, New Zealand), *A Voyage Round My Father* (Cambridge Theatre), *Long Day's Journey Into Night* (Young Vic & Cambridge Theatre), *Blood Wedding* (Lyric Theatre, Hammersmith), *Twelfth Night* (Everyman Playhouse, Liverpool), *Translations* (Royal Lyceum, Edinburgh), *The Darker Face of the Earth* (National Theatre). Mick Sands has also composed music for many productions at the Gate Theatre, Notting Hill, including the award-winning *Spanish Golden Age season, Hecuba, The Suppliants* and the *Agamemmnon's Children Trilogy*. He is a winner of he Christopher Whelen award for Music in Theatre.

Film: *American PBS* (Emmy Nomination*), Crescent* (Short film).

Television: *Tantalus: Behind the Mask.*

Radio: *Death & the King's Horsemen* (BBC Radio 3), *Iph* (BBC Radio 3 – Belfast).

GREGORY CLARKE Sound Designer

Theatre: West End & Broadway credits include: *The Vortex* (Apollo Theatre), *Ring Round The Moon* (Playhouse Theatre), *Cloud Nine* (Almeida Theatre), *Pygmalion* (American Airlines Theatre, Broadway), *Equus* (Gielgud and Broadway), *Journey's End* (London, UK tour and Broadway, New York Drama Desk Award winner for Outstanding Sound Design), *A Voyage Round My Father* (Wyndhams Theatre), *The Philanthropist* (Donmar Warehouse); *Hay Fever, Lady Windermere's Fan, The Royal Family* (Theatre Royal, Haymarket), *Honour* (Wyndhams Theatre), *The Home Place, Whose Life is it Anyway?* (Comedy Theatre), *The Emperor Jones* and *The Chairs* (Gate Theatre), *And Then There Were None, Some Girls* (Gielgud Theatre), *Waiting For Godot* (New Ambassadors Theatre), *What the Butler Saw* (Criterion Theatre), *The Dresser* (Duke Of York's Theatre), *Amy's View, You Never Can Tell* (Garrick), *National Anthems* (Old Vic); *Betrayal* (Duchess Theatre), *Abigail's Party* (New Ambassadors Theatre), *Mum's the Word* (Albery), *Song Of Singapore* (Mayfair Theatre), *No Man's Land, Tristan and Yseult, The Emperor Jones* (National Theatre), *Great Expectations, Coriolanus, The Merry Wives of Windsor, Tantalus* and *Cymbeline* (RSC).

Other Theatre credits include: *The New Electric Ballroom* (Druid, Galway and Edinburgh), *Troilus and Cressida* (European tour), *The English Game* (UK tour & Rose Theatre, Kingston), *Blackbird* (UK Tour, opening at Rose Theatre, Kingston), *Crown Matrimonial* (UK tour), *Uncle Vanya* (English Touring Theatre National Tour, opening at Rose Theatre, Kingston), *A Doll's House, Portrait of a Lady, Born In The Gardens, Pygmalion, Little Nell, Measure For Measure, Habeas Corpus, Miss Julie, Private Lives, Much Ado About Nothing, You Can Never Tell, Design for Living, Betrayal, Fight for Barbara, As You Like It* (The Peter Hall Company), *The Changeling* (Barbican), *Nights at the*

Circus (Lyric Theatre Hammersmith and tour), *Insignificance* (Sheffield Lyceum), *My Boy Jack* (UK tour), 6 Seasons at the Open Air Theatre, Regent's Park; *In The Club, Everything Is Illuminated, Clever Dick, The Schuman Plan, What the Butler Saw, When the Night Begins, Abigail's Party,* (Hampstead Theatre), *Seven Doors, Semi-Detached, Pal Joey, Heartbreak House, A Small Family Business, I Caught My Death in Venice, Nathan the Wise, Song of Singapore, Nymph Errant* (Chichester), *Office Suite, Present Laughter, Old Times, How The Other Half Loves, Victory* (Theatre Royal Bath).

JACKIE SNOW (née MATTHEWS) Movement Director

Theatre includes: *The Burial at Thebes* (Nottingham Playhouse, UK Tour, American Tour & Rose Theatre, Kingston), and numerous productions at the National Theatre, Royal Shakespeare Company, Northcott Theatre Exeter, Regents Park Theatre and Nottingham Playhouse.

Teaching: Jackie was Master of Movement at Shakespeare's Globe for three years, which included choreography, teaching and movement directing for the resident company. Other teaching includes credits at the London College of Dance and Drama, The Guildhall School of Music and Drama, The British American Drama Academy (London and Oxford programmes), LAMDA, Rose Bruford and Regents University. Jackie is currently Head of Movement at the Royal Academy of Dramatic Art.

Film and television includes: Stephen Poliakoff's *The Lost Prince, All Forgotten, Quills* and *The New World* (directed by Terrence Malick).

GEMMA HANCOCK & SAM STEVENSON Casting

Theatre includes: *The Portrait of a Lady, A Doll's House, The Vortex, Uncle Vanya, Pygmalion, Little Nell, Amy's View, Habeas Corpus, Measure for Measure, You Never Can Tell, Waiting for Godot, Much Ado About Nothing, The Dresser, As You Like It, Man & Superman* (all directed by Peter Hall), *In the Club, Honour, What the Butler Saw, Abigail's Party* (all directed by David Grindley), *Private Lives, Blithe Spirit, Don Juan, Tejas Verdes, Emperor Jones, The Chairs* (all directed by Thea Sharrock), *Ring Round The Moon* (directed by Sean Mathias), *The Deep Blue Sea* (directed by Edward Hall), *The Odyssey* (directed by David Farr), *Miss Julie, Everything is Illuminated* (directed by Rachel O'Riordan), *The Lieutenant of Inishmore* (directed by Wilson Milam), *Alice's Adventures in Wonderland, Beasts and Beauties, Watership Down* (directed by Melly Still) and *Ghosts* (directed by Anna Mackmin).

Film & Television includes: *Consuming Passion, Silent Witness, The Inspector Lynley Mysteries, Mr Loveday's Little Outing, Rough Crossings, The Romantics, Peter Ackroyd's London, The Bill, My Life as a Popat, Holby City, EastEnders, Babel* (UK Casting), *The New World* (Casting Associate).

THANK YOU

ROSE THEATRE
Kingston

Kingston Theatre Trust is grateful to the Royal Borough of Kingston Council and Kingston University, our many sponsors, donors, Friends and volunteers for their support in bringing the Rose Theatre project to fruition.

Sponsors
Frère Jacques

Patrons
Bentalls
HSBC
John Lewis Partnership
The New Victoria Hospital
Russell-Cooke Solicitors

Partners
Artifax Software Ltd
Carter Bells LLP Solicitors
Cattaneo Commercial
Clear Group
Kingston Readers Festival
Menzies Chartered Accountants
Opus Audio Technologies Ltd

Rose Associates
Anonymous
Stuart Baird
Will Bland & Tricia Welch Bland
Len Cowking
Michael & Mary Davison
Martin & Kathryn Higgs
Holland Hahn & Wills
Michael & Elizabeth Housden
Greg Hutchings
Pat Mackay
Pizza Express
Mick Sayer

Shrewsbury House School
Bob Steed
Systems Support UK Ltd t/a Copycare
Walker Dendle Financial Recruitment
Warren House
Elaine Elizabeth West

Members of the Director's Circle
Clive Butler
Professor John W Hunt
Iain More
Maxwell Morrsion
Ian Page
Lady Sainsbury of Turville
John & Vanessa Stone
Philip & Rosemary Swatman
Kevin & Sue Thomas
Brian Willman

Rose Circle Friends
John Arnold
In memory of Michael John Atherton
Michael Bagwell
Joe Bailey
Michael & Rosemary Bibby
John & Francine Brooks
Timothy Combe
Gail Cunningham
Timothy Doyle
Mr E F Field
John & Andrea Gabb
Peter Gray

Pam Harris
Peter Jarvis
Peter Juniper
Sophia & David Kester
In memory of Kenneth MacDonald
David Moore
Barry O'Mahony
Jean Pengelly
Donald Rogers
Kenneth & Rosalind Rokison
In memory of Marjorie Tassell
Jeremy Vines

Trusts and Foundations
Rowan Bentall Charitable Trust
The Mackintosh Foundation
The Golden Bottle Trust
The William Allen Young Charitable Trust
Reuben Foundation
The Tim Rice Charitable Trust
The Jam Trust
The Alchemy Foundation

Rose Friends
We would like to thank the large number of individuals who have supported the Rose Theatre, many of them with a continuing annual commitment.

FOUNDER FRIENDS

ROSE THEATRE
Kingston

We would like to give special thanks to the Founder Friends of the Rose Theatre, who gave their support long before the theatre became a reality.

Peter A Annett
Anonymous
Tony & Annette Anstee
Roy & Janet Balcomb
Elisabeth Barrett
Robyn Barton
Colin Bloxham
Andrew Bridge
Judy Bridgeman
Maureen Burnell
Tom Cairns & Janet Lee
Roger Chown & Amanda Shaw
Philip & Claire Cockle
Sylvia Cohen
Colemans-ctts Solicitors
Ronald Cook
Ian Coxon
In memory of Cllr Dilys Coy
Stephen & Penny D'Souza
Mr C R & Mrs R Dammers
Edward Davey MP
Nicola Davis
Michael & Mary Davison
Keith Day
Anthony Doulton
Timothy Doyle
Nigel Duffin
Richard Edgar
The Elmes Family
Alun & Bridget Evans
Roger Fairhead
Chris & Carrie Foulkes
Patricia Franks
Michael Frayn
Richard Freeborn
Mr & Mrs Freed
Marian Freedman

In memory of David Frett
Eric Gardner
Pat Garth
Mr C & Mrs C M Gill
Val Gooding CBE
Claude Green
Barbara Greenway
Cllr Sheila Griffin
Chris Gundry
John Hackett
John Kenneth Hadler
Roger & Andrea Hall
Sheila Hamilton
Baroness Sally Hamwee
Jan & the late Maurice Hanssen
Frances Hemus
Christine Heys
Martin & Kathryn Higgs
Glenda Hill
Erica Hirsch
Edna Hirschler
Peter Jarvis
Mrs J Jenkins
Bruce Jerrit
Andrew & Ruth Jones
Ross Jones
Elizabeth Kearns
In memory of Jo Keenan
Andrew Keene
In memory of Brenda Kempster
In memory of Helen Kidd
Irene Lappage
Jackie Latham
Eddie & Danny Lawson
Karin Lloyd
Ann Macfarlane MBE
Paul Maguire

Ralph Mason
Jenifer Matthew
William & Christine McMurray
Michael Philip Michaels
Sheila Millington
Barbara & Eric Mitchell
Sue Moller
Fiona Mongredien
Chris Moore
Feliks Morozgalski
Gloria Murphy
Maria Netley
James O'Keeffe
Linda Palmer
Tony & Carol Parker
Pearson Maddin Solicitors
Maureen Pianca
Mary Pollard & Bryan Boreham
Nick & Nicola Pratelli
Stephen & Celia Procter
Jill Raine
Philip & Jill Ralph
Katie Randerson
Cllrs Ian & Mary Reid
Benno & Jacqueline Reischel
Douglas G Reynolds
Rachael Reynolds
Mr J Ricketts
Peter Robinson
Jacqui Rollason
Alan Routs
Derrick Rowe, DPR Motorsport LLP
Jeannette Rowell
Brigadier F Rushmore CBE
Sinnathamby Sakthivel
Teri Scoble
Mandy Seffert

John Shea
Nick Sheldon & Leo Duff
Cllr Penny Shelton
Jacky Simon
Michael Smith
Fred & Margaret Squire
Andrew Stanley
Graham Stapleton
Cllr Bob Steed
Alan Stevenson
Elizabeth Sutter
Gillian Suttie
Linda Talmadge
Paul J Talman
Sheila Taylor
Helga Tidy
Jenny Titterton
Paul & Vivienne Tregenza
Anthony Tresigne
M-A Freshwater & J A Turner
Bridget Tyler
Mr & Mrs J Tyrer
Alan Vaughan
Nancy Vlasto
Mary Webb
Debra Westlake
Vicky Wilding
Mr & Mrs A & S Williams
Sandy Williams
Trevor Williams
Antonia Wilson
Frances Wilson
Dame Jacqueline Wilson
Derek & Valerie Winsor
Pat & Andrew Wislocki
Paul Wood
Katie Worsley
Peter & Susan Wright
Isobel Young

LOVE'S LABOUR'S LOST

BY WILLIAM SHAKESPEARE

A PERFORMING EDITION BY ROGER WARREN

First published in this edition in 2008 by Oberon Books Ltd
521 Caledonian Road, London N7 9RH
Tel: 020 7607 3637 / Fax: 020 7607 3629
e-mail: info@oberonbooks.com
www.oberonbooks.com

A catalogue record for this book is available from the British
Library.

ISBN: 978-1-84002-788-4

Cover artwork by Sarah Hyndman for With Relish

Printed in Great Britain by CPI Antony Rowe, Chippenham.

FROM NAVARRE TO WARWICKSHIRE:
LOVE'S LABOUR'S LOST

Peter Hall calls *Love's Labour's Lost* 'a celebration of Englishness'. Although Shakespeare based the central dramatic situation on an episode in French history, a ceremonial meeting in 1578-9 between a King of Navarre and a Princess of France to resolve a dispute over Aquitaine, as in the play, he anglicized these French aristocrats: Marshal Biron becomes Berowne, the Duc de Longueville Longaville, de la Mayenne Dumaine. Shakespeare seems to envisage the events of the play taking place, not in far-off Navarre, but in a park surrounding an Elizabethan great house, like Charlecote near Stratford. It is surely in such a setting, rather than in France, that we may expect to meet a constable named Anthony Dull.

Love's Labour's Lost is about the process of growing up. It is a journey to maturity, towards being ready for a lasting relationship – what the Princess, in a haunting phrase that Shakespeare also uses in one of his Sonnets, calls 'a world-without-end bargain'. The language of the play charts that journey, from the excesses of witty self-display to the simplicity of 'honest plain words', as Berowne calls them. But Berowne himself embodies both extremes. In his celebrated praise of love at the end of the sonnet-reading scene, his language rises to genuine eloquence: 'when love speaks, the voice of all the gods / Make heaven drowsy with the harmony.' But the dramatic context puts this eloquence into perspective. At the beginning of the play, the lords swear an oath to study for three years and to renounce the company of women; but when the ladies arrive on their political embassage, the lords break those oaths and set out to woo them. The keeping or breaking of oaths is thus a mainspring of the comedy. Vows solemnly taken cannot be simply set aside when it suits the lords to do so. They ask Berowne to justify their perjury; and his celebration of the power of love is thus part of a larger strategy, demonstrating that, since women 'are the books, the arts, the academes / That show, contain, and nourish all the world', the original vow to study is actually better observed by breaking than by keeping it. Ingenious, but sophistical, as Shakespeare makes clear when Berowne's argument culminates in the wittily contradictory phrase 'It is religion to be thus forsworn'.

But if the lords can break their vows of study so easily, how can the ladies believe their vows of love? This dilemma is heightened by a crisis: the entry of a black-clad messenger with the news that the Princess's father has died. This is one of the great *coups de théâtre* in Shakespeare. It is as if Death itself materializes on the stage, not only shattering the revels, but compelling everyone to abandon conventional phrases and to say just what they mean, and feel. The character most affected by the news, the Princess, reminds the King of his broken oath – 'your grace is perjured much' – but gives him the opportunity to redeem it: if he will genuinely retire from the world to a seclusion more demanding than his proposed Academe, she will believe his vows and accept his love. The other ladies impose similar penalties upon their suitors; Rosaline's terms to Berowne are especially tough, and they relate to the use and abuse of language that is so central to the play: 'A jest's prosperity lies in the ear / Of him that hears it, never in the tongue / Of him that makes it.' These penances are characteristic of Shakespearian comedy in placing wit and humour in a darker context: it is as if Shakespeare feels that the resolutions of comedy must be put to the test of harsher experience if they are to be convincing.

Even so, the play does not only end with death and parting, but also with the villagers' songs about the countryside in spring and winter – a different kind of reality. Shakespeare's anglicization of the court of Navarre is underlined by being set within an English country community. Several of these characters echo the court's infatuation with language, and they have their own kind of eloquence, as in Don Armado's farewell to arms or Holofernes' sheer relish of his pedantry. The final songs sustain, in a lyrical vein, the tough reality introduced by the messenger Mercadé in insisting on the mingling of pleasure and pain in the rural world. Amongst the delights of springtime, the cuckoo's cry sounds uncomfortably like 'cuckold' to married men – a light allusion to the tentative, conditional partnerships established by the court; and amid the discomforts of winter, the owl sings an unexpectedly 'merry' note. In striking a balance between sweet and sour in this way, the songs reinforce, not only the play's own balance of happiness and sadness, but that Englishness of which Peter Hall speaks.

Roger Warren

THIS EDITION

This performing text of *Love's Labour's Lost* was freshly prepared from the original, the Quarto of 1598, for Peter Hall's production at the Rose Theatre, Kingston, in 2008. The Quarto was almost certainly based on Shakespeare's manuscript, since it is full of the inconsistencies and confusions characteristic of a dramatist writing at speed without pausing to make corrections. The text of the play in the First Folio of Shakespeare's works (1623) was clearly based on the Quarto, since it reproduces some of the Quarto's printing errors; but it also introduces minor changes, suggesting that a separate manuscript, perhaps a prompt-book, was consulted. If so, this was done haphazardly, since major muddles in the Quarto survive in the Folio. But the Folio directions are fuller, and are often followed in this edition.

This text uses lighter punctuation than strictly grammatical modern usage would require, to preserve the shape and rhythm of the lines as much as possible, and to remove unnecessary obstacles to their speaking. I am very grateful to Angie Kendall for helping to prepare it.

Roger Warren

AN IDEAL STAGE FOR SHAKESPEARE

This production of *Love's Labour's Lost* is the first Shakespeare play to be specifically planned for the Rose, a stage that is ideally, indeed uniquely, suited to the purpose.

The Elizabethan Rose Theatre was built *c.* 1587 and somewhat altered in 1592. In 1989, during the demolition of a 1950s office block, its foundations were exposed. And there, amazingly, preserved in the London mud of four centuries, were some of the timbers of the Rose theatre stage – or rather, two stages, both the original and the 1592 modification. The shape of each was clearly visible; and it called into question received opinion of what the Elizabethan stage looked like.

Those theories were based, not on physical evidence such as had become available at the Rose, but on a pencil copy of a pencil sketch, done from memory in around 1596, of the Elizabethan Swan theatre, and on the contract for the Fortune theatre in 1599. This contract specified that the stage should 'extend to the middle of the yard of the said house'; and since it went on to say that 'the stage should be in all other proportions contrived and fashioned like unto the stage of … the Globe', it has been assumed that the Globe theatre had a thrust stage, extending deeply into the audience, particularly since that is what the sketch of the Swan seems to show. This is the assumption on which modern reconstructions of the Elizabethan stage – notably those at Stratford, Ontario, at the (modern) Swan in Stratford-upon-Avon, and at Shakespeare's Globe next door to the Rose site – are based. It must be emphasised that, although there is considerable pictorial evidence about the exterior of the original Globe theatre, there is no such evidence about what the interior was like; that is, we know quite a lot about the Globe except what matters most: the relation between actor and audience.

But for the Rose, evidence on this crucial point now exists – and it runs counter to the evidence of the Swan sketch and the Fortune contract. For the shape of the stage preserved by the Southwark mud was not a thrust but a lozenge: that is, wide and narrow, tapering towards the front. The entire audience was in front of the stage, not clustered around its sides, as in theatres with thrust stages. It is easy to see how the Restoration stage, and ultimately the proscenium stage, could have developed from such a model.

Advocates of the thrust stage argue that it enables the actor to get well forward, amongst the audience, and so increases communication with them. But there is a huge drawback to this view. When actors advance to the front of the thrust, they leave a significant proportion of the audience behind them. Those spectators are certainly not being communicated with. The thrust is also inflexible. At Stratford, Ontario, for example, there is only one point on the entire stage where the actor can stand in order to address the whole house, and that is well to the back, with the thrust yawning emptily in front, actually separating actor from audience.

While archaeology has revealed the most important fact about the Rose theatre, its stage, it cannot of course tell us much about the rest of the building – its height, the number of its galleries, and so on – and part of the site remains uncovered. Even so, standing on the excavated Rose stage and noting where the furthest walls of the theatre were, it was clear that an actor anywhere on this stage could communicate with the whole audience, because they were all in front of him: at the Rose, you can take in the entire house, something that is not possible in any of the reconstructions of the Globe theatre. We have here, therefore, the first practical recreation of an Elizabethan stage which is based on hard evidence, rather than on academic speculation.

But the Rose Theatre Kingston is not a space exclusively for staging Elizabethan drama; it can be used for any play of any period, while providing a special advantage over all existing ones for the staging of Shakespeare.

Roger Warren

Characters

THE KING OF NAVARRE

LONGAVILLE)

DUMAINE) his lords

BEROWNE)

DULL, a constable

COSTARD, a countryman

DON ADRIANO DE ARMADO, a Spanish braggart

MOTH, his page

JAQUENETTA, a dairymaid

THE PRINCESS OF FRANCE

BOYET, her chamberlain

MARIA)

KATHERINE) her ladies

ROSALINE)

A FORESTER

HOLOFERNES, a pedantic schoolmaster

SIR NATHANIEL, a curate

MERCADÉ, a royal messenger

SCENE ONE

Enter the KING OF NAVARRE, BEROWNE, LONGAVILLE, and DUMAINE

KING: Let fame, that all hunt after in their lives,
　　　Live registered upon our brazen tombs,
　　　And then grace us in the disgrace of death;
　　　When spite of cormorant devouring time,
　　　Th'endeavour of this present breath may buy
　　　That honour which shall bate his scythe's keen edge,
　　　And make us heirs of all eternity.
　　　Therefore brave conquerors, for so you are,
　　　That war against your own affections
　　　And the huge army of the world's desires,
　　　Our late edict shall strongly stand in force.
　　　Navarre shall be the wonder of the world.
　　　Our court shall be a little academe,
　　　Still and contemplative in living art.
　　　You three, Berowne, Dumaine, and Longaville,
　　　Have sworn for three years' term to live with me
　　　My fellow scholars, and to keep those statutes
　　　That are recorded in this schedule here.
　　　Your oaths are passed, and now subscribe your names,
　　　That his own hand may strike his honour down
　　　That violates the smallest branch herein.
　　　If you are armed to do as sworn to do,
　　　Subscribe to your deep oaths, and keep it too.

LONGAVILLE: I am resolved, 'tis but a three years' fast.
　　　The mind shall banquet though the body pine.
　　　Fat paunches have lean pates, and dainty bits
　　　Make rich the ribs but bankrupt quite the wits.

DUMAINE: My loving lord, Dumaine is mortified.
　　　The grosser manner of these world's delights
　　　He throws upon the gross world's baser slaves.
　　　To love, to wealth, to pomp, I pine and die,
　　　With all these living in philosophy.

BEROWNE: I can but say their protestation over,
 So much, dear liege, I have already sworn:
 That is, to live and study here three years.
 But there are other strict observances,
 As not to see a woman in that term,
 Which I hope well is not enrollèd there;
 And one day in a week to touch no food,
 And but one meal on every day beside,
 The which I hope is not enrollèd there;
 And then to sleep but three hours in the night,
 And not be seen to wink of all the day,
 When I was wont to think no harm all night,
 And make a dark night too of half the day,
 Which I hope well is not enrollèd there.
 O these are barren tasks, too hard to keep:
 Not to see ladies, study, fast, not sleep.

KING: Your oath is passed to pass away from these.

BEROWNE: Let me say no, my liege, an if you please.
 I only swore to study with your grace,
 And stay here in your court for three years' space.

LONGAVILLE: You swore to that, Berowne, and to the rest.

BEROWNE: By yea and nay sir, then I swore in jest.
 What is the end of study, let me know?

KING: Why, that to know which else we should not know.

BEROWNE: Things hid and barred, you mean, from common
 sense.

KING: Ay, that is study's god-like recompense.

BEROWNE: Come on then, I will swear to study so,
 To know the thing I am forbid to know,
 As thus: to study where I well may dine
 When I to feast expressly am forbid;
 Or study where to meet some mistress fine
 When mistresses from common sense are hid;
 Or having sworn too hard a keeping oath,

Study to break it and not break my troth.
If study's gain be thus, and this be so,
Study knows that which yet it doth not know.
Swear me to this, and I will ne'er say no.

KING: These be the stops that hinder study quite,
And train our intellects to vain delight.

BEROWNE: Why all delights are vain, but that most vain
Which with pain purchased doth inherit pain;
As painfully to pore upon a book
To seek the light of truth, while truth the while
Doth falsely blind the eyesight of his look.
Light seeking light doth light of light beguile;
So ere you find where light in darkness lies
Your light grows dark by losing of your eyes.
Study me how to please the eye indeed
By fixing it upon a fairer eye,
Who dazzling so, that eye shall be his heed,
And give him light that it was blinded by.
Study is like the heaven's glorious sun,
That will not be deep searched with saucy looks.
Small have continual plodders ever won
Save base authority from others' books.
These earthly godfathers of heaven's lights,
That give a name to every fixèd star,
Have no more profit of their shining nights
Than those that walk and wot not what they are.
Too much to know is to know naught but fame,
And every godfather can give a name.

KING: How well he's read, to reason against reading!

DUMAINE: Proceeded well, to stop all good proceeding.

LONGAVILLE: He weeds the corn and still lets grow the weeding.

BEROWNE: The spring is near when green geese are a-breeding.

DUMAINE: How follows that?

BEROWNE: Fit in his place and time.

33

DUMAINE: In reason nothing.

BEROWNE: Something then in rhyme.

KING: Berowne is like an envious sneaping frost,
     That bites the first-born infants of the spring.

BEROWNE: Well, say I am! Why should proud summer boast
     Before the birds have any cause to sing?
     Why should I joy in any abortive birth?
     At Christmas I no more desire a rose
     Than wish a snow in May's new-fangled shows,
     But like of each thing that in season grows.
     So you to study now it is too late,
     Climb o'er the house to unlock the little gate.

KING: Well, sit you out: go home Berowne, adieu.

BEROWNE: No my good lord, I have sworn to stay with you.
     And though I have for barbarism spoke more
     Than for that angel knowledge you can say,
     Yet confident I'll keep what I have sworn,
     And bide the penance of each three years' day.
     Give me the paper, let me read the same,
     And to the strict'st decrees I'll write my name.

KING: How well this yielding rescues thee from shame!

BEROWNE: '*Item*, that no woman shall come within a mile of my
     court.' Hath this been proclaimed?

LONGAVILLE: Four days ago.

BEROWNE: Let's see the penalty. 'On pain of losing her
     tongue.' Who devised this penalty?

LONGAVILLE: Marry, that did I.

BEROWNE: Sweet lord, and why?

LONGAVILLE: To fright them hence with that dread penalty.

BEROWNE: A dangerous law against gentility.

'*Item*, if any man be seen to talk with a woman within the
term of three years, he shall endure such public shame as
the rest of the court can possibly devise.'
This article, my liege, yourself must break,
For well you know here comes in embassy
The French King's daughter with yourself to speak,
A maid of grace and complete majesty,
About surrender up of Aquitaine
To her decrepit, sick, and bedrid father.
Therefore this article is made in vain,
Or vainly comes th'admirèd Princess hither.

KING: What say you lords? Why this was quite forgot.

BEROWNE: So study evermore is overshot.
  While it doth study to have what it would,
  It doth forget to do the thing it should;
  And when it hath the thing it hunteth most,
  'Tis won as towns with fire: so won, so lost.

KING: We must of force dispense with this decree.
  She must lie here on mere necessity.

BEROWNE: Necessity will make us all forsworn
  Three thousand times within this three years' space;
  For every man with his affects is born,
  Not by might mastered, but by special grace.
  If I break faith, this word shall speak for me:
  I am forsworn on mere necessity.
  So to the laws at large I write my name,
  And he that breaks them in the least degree
  Stands in attainder of eternal shame.
  Suggestions are to other as to me,
  But I believe, although I seem so loath,
  I am the last that will last keep his oath.
  But is there no quick recreation granted?

KING: Ay that there is. Our court you know is haunted
  With a refinèd traveller of Spain,
  A man in all the world's new fashion planted,
  That hath a mint of phrases in his brain:

One who the music of his own vain tongue
Doth ravish like enchanting harmony;
A man of contraries, whom right and wrong
Have chose as umpire of their mutiny.
This child of fancy, that Armado hight,
For interim to our studies shall relate
In high-borne words the worth of many a knight
From tawny Spain lost in the world's debate.
How you delight my lords, I know not I,
But I protest I love to hear him lie,
And I will use him for my minstrelsy.

BEROWNE: Armado is a most illustrious wight,
A man of fire-new words, fashion's own knight.

LONGAVILLE: Costard the swain and he shall be our sport,
And so to study three years is but short.

Enter Constable DULL, with COSTARD, with a letter

DULL: Which is the Duke's own person?

BEROWNE: This, fellow. What wouldst?

DULL: I myself reprehend his own person, for I am his grace's
farborough; but I would see his own person in flesh and
blood.

BEROWNE: This is he.

DULL: Signor Arm– Arm– commends you. There's villainy
abroad, this letter will tell you more.

COSTARD: Sir, the contempts thereof are as touching me.

KING: A letter from the magnificent Armado.

BEROWNE: How low soever the matter, I hope in God for
high words.

LONGAVILLE: A high hope for a low heaven. God grant us
patience.

BEROWNE: To hear, or forbear laughing?

LONGAVILLE: To hear meekly, sir, and to laugh moderately, or to forbear both.

BEROWNE: Well sir, be it as the style shall give us cause to climb in the merriness.

COSTARD: The matter is to me, sir, as concerning Jaquenetta. The manner of it is, I was taken with the manner.

BEROWNE: In what manner?

COSTARD: In manner and form following, sir, all those three. I was seen with her in the manor house, sitting with her upon the form, and taken following her into the park; which put together is in manner and form following. Now sir, for the manner: it is the manner of a man to speak to a woman. For the form: in some form.

BEROWNE: For the following, sir?

COSTARD: As it shall follow in my correction, and God defend the right.

KING: Will you hear this letter with attention?

BEROWNE: As we would hear an oracle.

COSTARD: Such is the simplicity of man to hearken after the flesh.

KING: 'Great deputy, the welkin's vicegerent and sole dominator of Navarre, my soul's earth's god, and body's fostering patron' –

COSTARD: Not a word of Costard yet.

KING: 'So it is' –

COSTARD: It may be so; but if he say it is so, he is in telling true, but so.

KING: Peace!

COSTARD: Be to me and every man that dares not fight.

KING: No words!

COSTARD: Of other men's secrets, I beseech you.

KING: 'So it is, besieged with sable-coloured melancholy, I
did commend the black-oppressing humour to the most
wholesome physic of thy health-giving air, and as I am a
gentleman, betook myself to walk. The time when? About
the sixth hour, when beasts most graze, birds best peck,
and men sit down to that nourishment which is called
supper. So much for the time when. Now for the ground
which – which I mean I walked upon. It is yclept thy park.
Then for the place where – where I mean I did encounter
that obscene and most preposterous event that draweth
from my snow-white pen the ebon-coloured ink which
here thou viewest, beholdest, surveyest, or seest. But to
the place where. It standeth north-north-east and by east
from the west corner of thy curious knotted garden. There
did I see that low-spirited swain, that base minnow of thy
mirth' –

COSTARD: Me?

KING: 'That unlettered, small-knowing soul' –

COSTARD: Me?

KING: 'That shallow vassal' –

COSTARD: Still me?

KING: 'Which as I remember, hight Costard' –

COSTARD: O, me!

KING: 'Sorted and consorted, contrary to thy established
proclaimed edict and continent canon, with, with, O with –
but with this I passion to say wherewith' –

COSTARD: With a wench.

KING: 'With a child of our grandmother Eve, a female, or
for thy more sweet understanding a woman. Him I, as
my ever-esteemed duty pricks me on, have sent to thee,

to receive the meed of punishment, by thy sweet grace's officer Anthony Dull, a man of good repute, carriage, bearing, and estimation.'

DULL: Me, an't shall please you. I am Anthony Dull.

KING: 'For Jaquenetta – so is the weaker vessel called – which I apprehended with the aforesaid swain, I keep her as a vessel of thy law's fury, and shall at the least of thy sweet notice bring her to trial. Thine in all compliments of devoted and heartburning heat of duty,
Don Adriano de Armado.'

BEROWNE: This is not so well as I looked for, but the best that ever I heard.

KING: Ay, the best for the worst. – But sirrah, what say you to this?

COSTARD: Sir, I confess the wench.

KING: Did you hear the proclamation?

COSTARD: I do confess much of the hearing it, but little of the marking of it.

KING: It was proclaimed a year's imprisonment to be taken with a wench.

COSTARD: I was taken with none, sir, I was taken with a damsel.

KING: Well, it was proclaimed damsel.

COSTARD: This was no damsel neither sir, she was a virgin.

KING: It is so varied too, for it was proclaimed virgin.

COSTARD: If it were, I deny her virginity. I was taken with a maid.

KING: This maid will not serve your turn, sir.

COSTARD: This maid will serve my turn, sir.

KING: Sir, I will pronounce your sentence: you shall fast a
    week with bran and water.

COSTARD: I had rather pray a month with mutton and
    porridge.

KING: And Don Armado shall be your keeper.
    My lord Berowne, see him delivered o'er,
    And go we lords, to put in practice that
    Which each to other hath so strongly sworn.
        Exeunt the KING, LONGAVILLE, and DUMAINE

BEROWNE: I'll lay my head to any good man's hat
    These oaths and laws will prove an idle scorn.
    Sirrah, come on.

COSTARD: I suffer for the truth sir; for true it is I was taken
    with Jaquenetta, and Jaquenetta is a true girl, and therefore
    welcome the sour cup of prosperity, affliction may one day
    smile again, and till then sit thee down sorrow.
        Exeunt

SCENE TWO

Enter ARMADO and MOTH, his page

ARMADO: Boy, what sign is it when a man of great spirit grows melancholy?

MOTH: A great sign, sir, that he will look sad.

ARMADO: Why, sadness is one and the selfsame thing, dear imp.

MOTH: No no, O Lord sir, no.

ARMADO: How canst thou part sadness and melancholy, my tender juvenal?

MOTH: By a familiar demonstration of the working, my tough signor.

ARMADO: Why tough signor, why tough signor?

MOTH: Why tender juvenal, why tender juvenal?

ARMADO: I spoke it, tender juvenal, as a congruent epitheton appertaining to thy young days, which we may nominate tender.

MOTH: And I, tough signor, as an appertinent title to your old time, which we may name tough.

ARMADO: Pretty and apt.

MOTH: How mean you sir? I pretty and my saying apt, or I apt and my saying pretty?

ARMADO: Thou pretty because little.

MOTH: Little pretty, because little. Wherefore apt?

ARMADO: And therefore apt because quick.

MOTH: Speak you this in my praise, master?

ARMADO: In thy condign praise.

MOTH: I will praise an eel with the same praise.

ARMADO: What, that an eel is ingenious?

MOTH: That an eel is quick.

ARMADO: I do say thou art quick in answers. Thou heat'st my blood.

MOTH: I am answered, sir.

ARMADO: I love not to be crossed.

MOTH: He speaks the mere contrary, crosses love not him.

ARMADO: I have promised to study three years with the Duke.

MOTH: You may do it in an hour, sir.

ARMADO: Impossible.

MOTH: How many is one, thrice told?

ARMADO: I am ill at reckoning, it fitteth the spirit of a tapster.

MOTH: You are a gentleman and a gamester, sir.

ARMADO: I confess both, they are both the varnish of a complete man.

MOTH: Then I am sure you know how much the gross sum of deuce-ace amounts to.

ARMADO: It doth amount to one more than two.

MOTH: Which the base vulgar do call three.

ARMADO: True.

MOTH: Why sir, is this such a piece of study? Now here is three studied ere you'll thrice wink, and how easy it is to put years to the word three, and study three years in two words, the dancing horse will tell you.

ARMADO: A most fine figure.

MOTH: To prove you a cipher.

ARMADO: I will hereupon confess I am in love; and as it
is base for a soldier to love, so am I in love with a base
wench. If drawing my sword against the humour of
affection would deliver me from the reprobate thought
of it, I would take desire prisoner and ransom him to any
French courtier for a new-devised courtesy. I think scorn to
sigh; methinks I should outswear Cupid. Comfort me, boy.
What great men have been in love?

MOTH: Hercules, master.

ARMADO: Most sweet Hercules! More authority, dear boy,
name more, and sweet my child, let them be men of good
repute and carriage.

MOTH: Samson, master; he was a man of good carriage, great
carriage, for he carried the town-gates on his back like a
porter, and he was in love.

ARMADO: O well-knit Samson, strong-jointed Samson! I
do excel thee in my rapier as much as thou didst me in
carrying gates. I am in love too. Who was Samson's love,
my dear Moth?

MOTH: A woman, master.

ARMADO: Of what complexion?

MOTH: Of all the four, or the three, or the two, or one of the
four.

ARMADO: Tell me precisely of what complexion?

MOTH: Of the sea-water green, sir.

ARMADO: Is that one of the four complexions?

MOTH: As I have read sir, and the best of them too.

ARMADO: Green indeed is the colour of lovers, but to have a
love of that colour, methinks Samson had small reason for
it. He surely affected her for her wit.

MOTH: It was so sir, for she had a green wit.

ARMADO: My love is most immaculate white and red.

MOTH: Most maculate thoughts, master, are masked under such colours.

ARMADO: Define, define, well-educated infant.

MOTH: My father's wit and my mother's tongue assist me!

ARMADO: Sweet invocation of a child, most pretty and pathetical.

MOTH: If she be made of white and red
    Her faults will ne'er be known,
    For blushing cheeks by faults are bred,
    And fears by pale white shown.
    Then if she fear or be to blame,
    By this you shall not know;
    For still her cheeks possess the same
    Which native she doth owe.
    A dangerous rhyme, master, against the reason of white and red.

ARMADO: Is there not a ballad, boy, of the King and the Beggar?

MOTH: The world was very guilty of such a ballad some three ages since, but I think now 'tis not to be found; or if it were, it would neither serve for the writing nor the tune.

ARMADO: I will have that subject newly writ o'er, that I may example my digression by some mighty precedent. Boy, I do love that country girl that I took in the park with the rational hind Costard; she deserves well.

MOTH: To be whipped – and yet a better love than my master.

ARMADO: Sing boy, my spirit grows heavy in love.

MOTH: And that's great marvel, loving a light wench.

ARMADO: I say sing.

MOTH: Forbear till this company be past.

*Enter COSTARD the Clown, Constable DULL, and
JAQUENETTA, a wench*

DULL: Sir, the Duke's pleasure is that you keep Costard
safe, and you must suffer him to take no delight, nor no
penance, but he must fast three days a week. For this
damsel, I must keep her at the park, she is allowed for the
dairy-woman. Fare you well.

ARMADO: I do betray myself with blushing. – Maid.

JAQUENETTA: Man.

ARMADO: I will visit thee at the lodge.

JAQUENETTA: That's hereby.

ARMADO: I know where it is situate.

JAQUENETTA: Lord, how wise you are!

ARMADO: I will tell thee wonders.

JAQUENETTA: With that face?

ARMADO: I love thee.

JAQUENETTA: So I heard you say.

ARMADO: And so farewell.

JAQUENETTA: Fair weather after you.

DULL: Come Jaquenetta, away.

Exeunt DULL and JAQUENETTA

ARMADO: Villain, thou shalt fast for thy offences ere thou be
pardoned.

COSTARD: Well sir, I hope when I do it I shall do it on a full
stomach.

ARMADO: Thou shalt be heavily punished.

COSTARD: I am more bound to you than your fellows, for they
are but lightly rewarded.

ARMADO: Take away this villain, shut him up.

MOTH: Come, you transgressing slave, away!

COSTARD: Let me not be pent up sir, I will fast being loose.

MOTH: No sir, that were fast and loose: thou shalt to prison.

COSTARD: Well, if ever I do see the merry days of desolation that I have seen, some shall see.

MOTH: What shall some see?

COSTARD: Nay nothing, Master Moth, but what they look upon. It is not for prisoners to be too silent in their words, and therefore I will say nothing. I thank God I have as little patience as another man, and therefore I can be quiet.

Exeunt MOTH and COSTARD

ARMADO: I do affect the very ground, which is base, where her shoe, which is baser, guided by her foot, which is basest, doth tread. I shall be forsworn, which is a great argument of falsehood, if I love. And how can that be true love which is falsely attempted? Love is a familiar, love is a devil; there is no evil angel but love. Yet was Samson so tempted, and he had an excellent strength; yet was Solomon so seduced, and he had a very good wit. Cupid's butt-shaft is too hard for Hercules' club, and therefore too much odds for a Spaniard's rapier. The first and second cause will not serve my turn: the passado he respects not, the duello he regards not; his disgrace is to be called boy, but his glory is to subdue men. Adieu valour, rust rapier, be still drum, for your manager is in love; yea, he loveth. Assist me some extemporal god of rhyme, for I am sure I shall turn sonnet. Devise wit, write pen, for I am for whole volumes in folio.

Exit

SCENE THREE

*Enter the PRINCESS OF FRANCE with three attending ladies,
MARIA, KATHERINE, and ROSALINE, BOYET, and two Lords*

BOYET: Now madam, summon up your dearest spirits.
    Consider who the King your father sends,
    To whom he sends, and what's his embassy:
    Yourself, held precious in the world's esteem,
    To parley with the sole inheritor
    Of all perfections that a man may owe,
    Matchless Navarre; the plea of no less weight
    Than Aquitaine, a dowry for a queen.
    Be now as prodigal of all dear grace
    As nature was in making graces dear
    When she did starve the general world beside
    And prodigally gave them all to you.

PRINCESS: Good Lord Boyet, my beauty, though but mean,
    Needs not the painted flourish of your praise.
    Beauty is bought by judgement of the eye,
    Not uttered by base sale of chapmen's tongues.
    I am less proud to hear you tell my worth
    Than you much willing to be counted wise
    In spending your wit in the praise of mine.
    But now to task the tasker: good Boyet,
    You are not ignorant all-telling fame
    Doth noise abroad Navarre hath made a vow
    Till painful study shall outwear three years
    No woman may approach his silent court.
    Therefore to us seemeth it a needful course,
    Before we enter his forbidden gates,
    To know his pleasure, and in that behalf,
    Bold of your worthiness, we single you
    As our best-moving fair solicitor:
    Tell him the daughter of the King of France,
    On serious business craving quick dispatch,
    Importunes personal conference with his grace.
    Haste, signify so much while we attend,
    Like humble-visaged suitors, his high will.

BOYET: Proud of employment, willingly I go.

PRINCESS: All pride is willing pride, and yours is so.

Exit BOYET

Who are the votaries, my loving lords,
That are vow-fellows with this virtuous duke?

KATHERINE: Lord Longaville is one.

PRINCESS: Know you the man?

MARIA: I know him, madam. At a marriage feast
Between Lord Perigord and the beauteous heir
Of Jaques Falconbridge solemnizèd
In Normandy saw I this Longaville.
A man of sovereign parts he is esteemed,
Well fitted in arts, glorious in arms.
Nothing becomes him ill that he would well.
The only soil of his fair virtue's gloss,
If virtue's gloss will stain with any soil,
Is a sharp wit matched with too blunt a will,
Whose edge hath power to cut, whose will still wills
It should none spare that come within his power.

PRINCESS: Some merry mocking lord belike, is't so?

MARIA: They say so most that most his humours know.

PRINCESS: Such short-lived wits do wither as they grow.
Who are the rest?

KATHERINE: The young Dumaine, a well-accomplished youth,
Of all that virtue love for virtue loved,
Most power to do most harm, least knowing ill,
For he hath wit to make an ill shape good,
And shape to win grace, though he had no wit.
I saw him at the Duke Alanson's once,
And much too little of that good I saw
Is my report to his great worthiness.

ROSALINE: Another of these students at that time
Was there with him, if I have heard a truth.

Berowne they call him, but a merrier man,
Within the limit of becoming mirth,
I never spent an hour's talk withal.
His eye begets occasion for his wit,
For every object that the one doth catch
The other turns to a mirth-moving jest,
Which his fair tongue, conceit's expositor,
Delivers in such apt and gracious words
That agèd ears play truant at his tales,
And younger hearings are quite ravishèd,
So sweet and voluble is his discourse.

PRINCESS: God bless my ladies, are they all in love,
That every one her own hath garnishèd
With such bedecking ornaments of praise?

MARIA: Here comes Boyet.

Enter BOYET

PRINCESS: Now, what admittance, lord?

BOYET: Navarre had notice of your fair approach,
And he and his competitors in oath
Were all addressed to meet you, gentle lady,
Before I came. Marry, thus much I have learnt:
He rather means to lodge you in the field,
Like one that comes here to besiege his court,
Than seek a dispensation for his oath
To let you enter his unpeopled house.

Enter the KING, LONGAVILLE, DUMAINE, and BEROWNE

Here comes Navarre.

KING: Fair Princess, welcome to the court of Navarre.

PRINCESS: Fair I give you back again, and welcome I have
not yet: the roof of this court is too high to be yours, and
welcome to the wide fields too base to be mine.

KING: You shall be welcome, madam, to my court.

PRINCESS: I will be welcome then, conduct me thither.

KING: Hear me dear lady, I have sworn an oath –

PRINCESS: Our Lady help my lord, he'll be forsworn.

KING: Not for the world, fair madam, by my will.

PRINCESS: Why, will shall break it, will and nothing else.

KING: Your ladyship is ignorant what it is.

PRINCESS: Were my lord so, his ignorance were wise,
Where now his knowledge must prove ignorance.
I hear your grace hath sworn out housekeeping.
'Tis deadly sin to keep that oath, my lord,
And sin to break it.
But pardon me, I am too sudden-bold,
To teach a teacher ill beseemeth me.
Vouchsafe to read the purpose of my coming,
And suddenly resolve me in my suit.

KING: Madam I will, if suddenly I may.

PRINCESS: You will the sooner that I were away,
For you'll prove perjured if you make me stay.

BEROWNE: Did not I dance with you in Brabant once?

ROSALINE: Did not I dance with you in Brabant once?

BEROWNE: I know you did.

ROSALINE: How needless was it then
To ask the question!

BEROWNE: You must not be so quick.

ROSALINE: 'Tis 'long of you, that spur me with such questions.

BEROWNE: Your wit's too hot, it speeds too fast, 'twill tire.

ROSALINE: Not till it leave the rider in the mire.

BEROWNE: What time o' day?

ROSALINE: The hour that fools should ask.

BEROWNE: Now fair befall your mask.

ROSALINE: Fair fall the face it covers.

BEROWNE: And send you many lovers.

ROSALINE: Amen, so you be none.

BEROWNE: Nay then will I be gone.

KING: Madam, your father here doth intimate
    The payment of a hundred thousand crowns,
    Being but the one half of an entire sum
    Disbursèd by my father in his wars.
    But say that he or we, as neither have,
    Received that sum, yet there remains unpaid
    A hundred thousand more, in surety of the which
    One part of Aquitaine is bound to us,
    Although not valued to the money's worth.
    If then the King your father will restore
    But that one half which is unsatisfied,
    We will give up our right in Aquitaine
    And hold fair friendship with his majesty.
    But that it seems he little purposeth,
    For here he doth demand to have repaid
    A hundred thousand crowns, and not demands,
    On payment of a hundred thousand crowns,
    To have his title live in Aquitaine,
    Which we much rather had depart withal,
    And have the money by our father lent,
    Than Aquitaine, so gelded as it is.
    Dear Princess, were not his requests so far
    From reason's yielding, your fair self should make
    A yielding 'gainst some reason in my breast,
    And go well satisfied to France again.

PRINCESS: You do the King my father too much wrong,
    And wrong the reputation of your name,
    In so unseeming to confess receipt
    Of that which hath so faithfully been paid.

KING: I do protest I never heard of it;
    And if you prove it I'll repay it back
    Or yield up Aquitaine.

PRINCESS: We arrest your word.
    Boyet, you can produce acquittances
    For such a sum from special officers
    Of Charles his father.

KING: Satisfy me so.

BOYET: So please your grace, the packet is not come
    Where that and other specialties are bound.
    Tomorrow you shall have a sight of them.

KING: It shall suffice me, at which interview
    All liberal reason I will yield unto.
    Meantime receive such welcome at my hand
    As honour, without breach of honour, may
    Make tender of to thy true worthiness.
    You may not come, fair princess, within my gates,
    But here without you shall be so received
    As you shall deem yourself lodged in my heart,
    Though so denied fair harbour in my house.
    Your own good thoughts excuse me, and farewell.
    Tomorrow shall we visit you again.

PRINCESS: Sweet health and fair desires consort your grace.

KING: Thy own wish wish I thee in every place.
                      Exit with LONGAVILLE and DUMAINE

BEROWNE: Lady, I will commend you to my own heart.

ROSALINE: Pray you do my commendations, I would be glad
    to see it.

BEROWNE: I would you heard it groan.

ROSALINE: Is the fool sick?

BEROWNE: Sick at the heart.

ROSALINE: Alack, let it blood.

BEROWNE: Would that do it good?

ROSALINE: My physic says ay.

BEROWNE: Will you prick't with your eye?

ROSALINE: No point, with my knife.

BEROWNE: Now God save thy life.

ROSALINE: And yours, from long living.

BEROWNE: I cannot stay thanksgiving.

Exit

Enter DUMAINE

DUMAINE: (*To BOYET*) Sir, I pray you a word. What lady
is that same?

BOYET: The heir of Alanson, Katherine her name.

DUMAINE: A gallant lady. Monsieur, fare you well.

Exit

Enter LONGAVILLE

LONGAVILLE: (*To BOYET*) I beseech you a word, what is she in
the white?

BOYET: A woman sometimes, if you saw her in the light.

LONGAVILLE: Perchance light in the light: I desire her name.

BOYET: She hath but one for herself, to desire that were a shame.

LONGAVILLE: Pray you sir, whose daughter?

BOYET: Her mother's, I have heard.

LONGAVILLE: God's blessing on your beard!

BOYET: Good sir, be not offended.
She is an heir of Falconbridge.

LONGAVILLE: Nay, my choler is ended.
She is a most sweet lady.

BOYET: Not unlike, sir, that may be.

Exit LONGAVILLE

Enter BEROWNE

BEROWNE: What's her name in the cap?

BOYET: Rosaline, by good hap.

BEROWNE: Is she wedded or no?

BOYET: To her will, sir, or so.

BEROWNE: O you are welcome sir, adieu.

BOYET: Farewell to me sir, and welcome to you.

Exit BEROWNE

MARIA: That last is Berowne, the merry madcap lord.
    Not a word with him but a jest.

BOYET: And every jest but a word.

PRINCESS: It was well done of you to take him at his word.

BOYET: I was as willing to grapple as he was to board.

KATHERINE: Two hot sheeps, marry.

BOYET: And wherefore not ships?
    No sheep, sweet lamb, unless we feed on your lips.

KATHERINE: You sheep and I pasture: shall that finish the jest?

BOYET: So you grant pasture for me.

KATHERINE: Not so, gentle beast.
    My lips are no common, though several they be.

BOYET: Belonging to whom?

KATHERINE: To my fortunes and me.

PRINCESS: Good wits will be jangling, but gentles agree.
    This civil war of wits were much better used
    On Navarre and his bookmen, for here 'tis abused.

BOYET: If my observation, which very seldom lies,
    By the heart's still rhetoric disclosèd with eyes,
    Deceive me not now, Navarre is infected.

PRINCESS: With what?

BOYET: With that which we lovers entitle 'affected'.

PRINCESS: Your reason?

BOYET: Why, all his behaviours did make their retire
    To the court of his eye, peeping thorough desire.
    His heart like an agate with your print impressed,
    Proud with his form, in his eye pride expressed.
    His tongue, all impatient to speak and not see,
    Did stumble with haste in his eyesight to be.
    All senses to that sense did make their repair,
    To feel only looking on fairest of fair.
    Methought all his senses were locked in his eye,
    As jewels in crystal for some prince to buy,
    Who tend'ring their own worth from where they were
        glassed,
    Did point you to buy them along as you passed.
    His face's own margin did quote such amazes
    That all eyes saw his eyes enchanted with gazes.
    I'll give you Aquitaine and all that is his
    An you give him for my sake but one loving kiss.

PRINCESS: Come to our pavilion, Boyet is disposed.

BOYET: But to speak that in words which his eye hath disclosed.
    I only have made a mouth of his eye
    By adding a tongue which I know will not lie.

ROSALINE: Thou art an old love-monger, and speak'st skilfully.

MARIA: He is Cupid's grandfather, and learns news of him.

KATHERINE: Then was Venus like her mother, for her father is
    but grim.

BOYET: Do you hear, my mad wenches?

MARIA: No.

BOYET: What then, do you see?

KATHERINE: Ay, our way to be gone.

BOYET: You are too hard for me.

Exeunt

SCENE FOUR

Enter ARMADO the braggart, and MOTH his boy

ARMADO: Warble, child, make passionate my sense of
hearing.

MOTH: (*Sings*) Concolinel.

ARMADO: Sweet air! Go tenderness of years, take this key,
give enlargement to the swain, bring him festinately hither,
I must employ him in a letter to my love.

MOTH: Master, will you win your love with a French brawl?

ARMADO: How meanest thou, brawling in French?

MOTH: No my complete master, but to jig off a tune at the
tongue's end, canary to it with your feet, humour it with
turning up your eyelids, sigh a note and sing a note,
sometime through the throat as if you swallowed love
with singing love, sometime through the nose as if you
snuffed up love by smelling love, with your hat penthouse-
like o'er the shop of your eyes, with your arms crossed
on your thin-belly doublet like a rabbit on a spit, or your
hands in your pocket like a man after the old painting,
and keep not too long in one tune, but a snip and away.
These are compliments, these are humours, these betray
nice wenches that would be betrayed without these, and
make them men of note – do you note me? – that most are
affected to these.

ARMADO: How hast thou purchased this experience?

MOTH: By my penny of observation.

ARMADO: But O, but O –

MOTH: The hobby-horse is forgot.

ARMADO: Call'st thou my love hobby-horse?

MOTH: No master, the hobby-horse is but a colt, and your love
perhaps a hackney. But have you forgot your love?

ARMADO: Almost I had.

MOTH: Negligent student, learn her by heart.

ARMADO: By heart and in heart, boy.

MOTH: And out of heart, master: all those three I will prove.

ARMADO: What wilt thou prove?

MOTH: A man, if I live; and this, by, in, and without, upon the instant: by heart you love her because your heart cannot come by her; in heart you love her because your heart is in love with her; and out of heart you love her, being out of heart that you cannot enjoy her.

ARMADO: I am all these three.

MOTH: And three times as much more, and yet nothing at all.

ARMADO: Fetch hither the swain, he must carry me a letter.

MOTH: A message well sympathized, a horse to be ambassador for an ass.

ARMADO: Ha ha, what sayst thou?

MOTH: Marry sir, you must send the ass upon the horse, for he is very slow-gaited; but I go.

ARMADO: The way is but short, away!

MOTH: As swift as lead, sir.

ARMADO: The meaning, pretty ingenious?
Is not lead a metal heavy, dull, and slow?

MOTH: *Minime*, honest master, or rather, master, no.

ARMADO: I say lead is slow.

MOTH: You are too swift, sir, to say so.
Is that lead slow which is fired from a gun?

ARMADO: Sweet smoke of rhetoric!
He reputes me a cannon, and the bullet, that's he.

I shoot thee at the swain.

MOTH: Thump then, and I flee.

Exit

ARMADO: A most acute juvenal, voluble and free of grace.
By thy favour, sweet welkin, I must sigh in thy face.
Most rude melancholy, valour gives thee place.
My herald is returned.

Enter MOTH the page, and COSTARD the clown

MOTH: A wonder, master: here's a costard broken in a shin.

ARMADO: Some enigma, some riddle; come, thy l'envoy begin.

COSTARD: No egma, no riddle, no l'envoy, no salve in the
mail, sir. O sir, plantain, a plain plantain: no l'envoy, no
l'envoy, no salve, sir, but a plantain.

ARMADO: By virtue, thou enforcest laughter, thy silly thought
my spleen. The heaving of my lungs provokes me to
ridiculous smiling. O pardon me, my stars! Doth the
inconsiderate take salve for l'envoy, and the word l'envoy
for a salve?

MOTH: Do the wise think them other? Is not l'envoy a salve?

ARMADO: No page, it is an epilogue or discourse to make plain
Some obscure precedence that hath tofore been sain.
I will example it.
    The fox, the ape, and the humble-bee
    Were still at odds, being but three.
There's the moral: now the l'envoy.

MOTH: I will add the l'envoy, say the moral again.

ARMADO: The fox, the ape, and the humble-bee
    Were still at odds, being but three.

MOTH: Until the goose came out of door
    And stayed the odds by adding four.
Now will I begin your moral, and do you follow with my
l'envoy.

> The fox, the ape, and the humble-bee
> Were still at odds, being but three.

ARMADO: Until the goose came out of door,
> Staying the odds by adding four.

MOTH: A good l'envoy, ending in the goose: would you desire more?

COSTARD: The boy hath sold him a bargain, a goose, that's flat.
Sir, your pennyworth is good an your goose be fat.
To sell a bargain well is as cunning as fast and loose.
Let me see a fat l'envoy, ay that's a fat goose.

ARMADO: Come hither, come hither. How did this argument begin?

MOTH: By saying that a costard was broken in a shin.
Then called you for the l'envoy.

COSTARD: True, and I for a plantain, thus came your argument in, then the boy's fat l'envoy, the goose that you bought, and he ended the market.

ARMADO: But tell me, how was there a costard broken in a shin?

MOTH: I will tell you sensibly.

COSTARD: Thou hast no feeling of it Moth, I will speak that l'envoy:
I Costard running out, that was safely within,
Fell over the threshold and broke my shin.

ARMADO: We will talk no more of this matter.

COSTARD: Till there be more matter in the shin.

ARMADO: Sirrah Costard, I will enfranchise thee.

COSTARD: O marry me to one Frances! I smell some l'envoy, some goose, in this.

ARMADO: By my sweet soul, I mean setting thee at liberty,
    enfreedoming thy person. Thou wert immured, restrained,
    captivated, bound.

COSTARD: True, true, and now you will be my purgation and
    let me loose.

ARMADO: I give thee thy liberty, set thee from durance,
    and in lieu thereof impose on thee nothing but this: bear
    this significant to the country maid Jaquenetta. There
    is remuneration, for the best ward of mine honour is
    rewarding my dependants. Moth, follow.

Exit

MOTH: Like the sequel I. Signor Costard adieu.

Exit

COSTARD: My sweet ounce of man's flesh, my incony Jew!
    Now will I look to his remuneration. Remuneration: O
    that's the Latin word for three-farthings. Three- farthings:
    remuneration. 'What's the price of this inkle?' 'One
    penny.' 'No, I'll give you a remuneration.' Why it carries it!
    Remuneration! Why it is a fairer name than French crown.
    I will never buy and sell out of this word.

Enter BEROWNE

BEROWNE: My good knave Costard, exceedingly well met.

COSTARD: Pray you sir, how much carnation ribbon may a
    man buy for a remuneration?

BEROWNE: What is a remuneration?

COSTARD: Marry sir, halfpenny-farthing.

BEROWNE: Why then, three-farthing-worth of silk.

COSTARD: I thank your worship, God be wi' you.

BEROWNE: Stay slave, I must employ thee.
    As thou wilt win my favour, good my knave,
    Do one thing for me that I shall entreat.

COSTARD: When would you have it done, sir?

BEROWNE: This afternoon.

COSTARD: Well, I will do it sir, fare you well.

BEROWNE: Thou knowest not what it is.

COSTARD: I shall know sir, when I have done it.

BEROWNE: Why villain, thou must know first.

COSTARD: I will come to your worship tomorrow morning.

BEROWNE: It must be done this afternoon.
    Hark slave, it is but this:
    The Princess comes to hunt here in the park,
    And in her train there is a gentle lady.
    When tongues speak sweetly, then they name her name,
    And Rosaline they call her, ask for her,
    And to her white hand see thou do commend
    This sealed-up counsel. There's thy guerdon, go.

COSTARD: Gardon! O sweet gardon, better than
    remuneration, elevenpence-farthing better; most sweet
    gardon! I will do it sir, in print. Gardon; remuneration.
                                        Exit

BEROWNE: And I forsooth in love, I that have been love's whip,
    A very beadle to a humorous sigh,
    A critic, nay a night-watch constable,
    A domineering pedant o'er the boy,
    Than whom no mortal so magnificent.
    This wimpled, whining, purblind, wayward boy,
    This Signor Junior, giant dwarf, Dan Cupid,
    Regent of love-rhymes, lord of folded arms,
    Th'anointed sovereign of sighs and groans,
    Liege of all loiterers and malcontents,
    Dread prince of plackets, king of codpieces,
    Sole imperator and great general
    Of trotting paritors – O my little heart!
    And I to be a corporal of his field,

And wear his colours like a tumbler's hoop!
What, I love, I sue, I seek a wife,
A woman that is like a German clock,
Still a-repairing, ever out of frame,
And never going aright, being a watch,
But being watched that it may still go right.
Nay to be perjured, which is worst of all,
And among three to love the worst of all:
A whitely wanton with a velvet brow,
With two pitch-balls stuck in her face for eyes –
Ay and by heaven, one that will do the deed
Though Argus were her eunuch and her guard.
And I to sigh for her, to watch for her,
To pray for her – go to, it is a plague
That Cupid will impose for my neglect
Of his almighty dreadful little might.
Well, I will love, write, sigh, pray, sue, and groan:
Some men must love my lady, and some Joan.

Exit

SCENE FIVE

Enter the PRINCESS, BOYET, a FORESTER, her Ladies and her Lords

PRINCESS: Was that the King that spurred his horse so hard
    Against the steep uprising of the hill?

BOYET: I know not, but I think it was not he.

PRINCESS: Whoe'er he was, he showed a mounting mind.
    Well lords, today we shall have our dispatch.
    On Saturday we will return to France.
    Then forester my friend, where is the bush
    That we must stand and play the murderer in?

FORESTER: Hereby, upon the edge of yonder coppice,
    A stand where you may make the fairest shoot.

PRINCESS: I thank my beauty, I am fair that shoot,
    And thereupon thou speak'st the fairest shoot.

FORESTER: Pardon me madam, for I meant not so.

PRINCESS: What, what? First praise me, and again say no?
    O short-lived pride! Not fair? Alack for woe!

FORESTER: Yes madam, fair.

PRINCESS: Nay, never paint me now.
    Where fair is not, praise cannot mend the brow.
    Here good my glass, take this for telling true.
    Fair payment for foul words is more than due.

FORESTER: Nothing but fair is that which you inherit.

PRINCESS: See see, my beauty will be saved by merit!
    O heresy in fair, fit for these days:
    A giving hand, though foul, shall have fair praise.
    But come, the bow. Now mercy goes to kill,
    And shooting well is then accounted ill.
    Thus will I save my credit in the shoot:
    Not wounding, pity would not let me do't;
    If wounding, then it was to show my skill,

That more for praise than purpose meant to kill.
And out of question, so it is sometimes:
Glory grows guilty of detested crimes,
When for fame's sake, for praise, an outward part,
We bend to that the working of the heart,
As I for praise alone now seek to spill
The poor deer's blood that my heart means no ill.

BOYET: Do not curst wives hold that self-sovereignty
  Only for praise' sake when they strive to be
  Lords o'er their lords?

PRINCESS: Only for praise, and praise we may afford
  To any lady that subdues a lord.

Enter COSTARD the clown

BOYET: Here comes a member of the commonwealth.

COSTARD: God dig-you-den all. Pray you, which is the head
  lady?

PRINCESS: Thou shalt know her, fellow, by the rest that have
  no heads.

COSTARD: Which is the greatest lady, the highest?

PRINCESS: The thickest and the tallest.

COSTARD: The thickest and the tallest: it is so, truth is truth.
  An your waist, mistress, were as slender as my wit,
  One o' these maids' girdles for your waist should be fit.
  Are not you the chief woman? You are the thickest here.

PRINCESS: What's your will sir, what's your will?

COSTARD: I have a letter from Monsieur Berowne to one
  Lady Rosaline.

PRINCESS: O thy letter, thy letter, he's a good friend of mine.
  Stand aside, good bearer. Boyet, you can carve,
  Break up this capon.

BOYET: I am bound to serve.

This letter is mistook; it importeth none here.
It is writ to Jaquenetta.

PRINCESS: We will read it, I swear.
Break the neck of the wax, and everyone give ear.

BOYET: (*Reads*) 'By heaven, that thou art fair is most infallible,
true that thou art beauteous, truth itself that thou art lovely.
More fairer than fair, beautiful than beauteous, truer than
truth itself, have commiseration on thy heroical vassal. The
magnanimous and most illustrate King Cophetua set eye
upon the penurious and indubitate beggar Zenelophon,
and he it was that might rightly say *Veni, vidi, vici*, which
to annothanize in the vulgar – O base and obscure vulgar!
– *videlicet*, He came, saw, and overcame. He came, one;
saw, two; overcame, three. Who came? The King. Why
did he come? To see. Why did he see? To overcome. To
whom came he? To the beggar. What saw he? The beggar.
Who overcame he? The beggar. The conclusion is victory.
On whose side? The King's. The captive is enriched. On
whose side? The beggar's. The catastrophe is a nuptial. On
whose side? The King's – no, on both in one, or one in
both. I am the King, for so stands the comparison; thou the
beggar, for so witnesseth thy lowliness. Shall I command
thy love? I may. Shall I enforce thy love? I could. Shall I
entreat thy love? I will. What shalt thou exchange for rags?
Robes. For tittles? Titles. For thyself? Me. Thus expecting
thy reply, I profane my lips on thy foot, my eyes on thy
picture, and my heart on thy every part.
Thine in the dearest design of industry,
Don Adriano de Armado.
Thus dost thou hear the Nemean lion roar
'Gainst thee, thou lamb, that standest as his prey.
Submissive fall his princely feet before,
And he from forage will incline to play.
But if thou strive, poor soul, what art thou then?
Food for his rage, repasture for his den.'

PRINCESS: What plume of feathers is he that indited this letter?
What vane, what weathercock? Did you ever hear better?

BOYET: I am much deceived but I remember the style.

PRINCESS: Else your memory is bad, going o'er it erewhile.

BOYET: This Armado is a Spaniard that keeps here in court,
 A phantasim, a Monarcho, and one that makes sport
 To the Prince and his bookmates.

PRINCESS: Thou fellow, a word.
 Who gave thee this letter?

COSTARD: I told you, my lord.

PRINCESS: To whom shouldst thou give it?

COSTARD: From my lord to my lady.

PRINCESS: From which lord to which lady?

COSTARD: From my lord Berowne, a good master of mine,
 To a lady of France that he called Rosaline.

PRINCESS: Thou hast mistaken his letter. Come lords, away.
 – Here, sweet, put up this, 'twill be thine another day.
           Exit attended

BOYET: Who is the shooter? Who is the suitor?

ROSALINE: Shall I teach you to know?

BOYET: Ay, my continent of beauty.

ROSALINE: Why she that bears the bow.
 Finely put off.

BOYET: My lady goes to kill horns, but if thou marry,
 Hang me by the neck if horns that year miscarry.
 Finely put on.

ROSALINE: Well then, I am the shooter.

BOYET: And who is your deer?

ROSALINE: If we choose by the horns, yourself come not near.
 Finely put on indeed!

MARIA: You still wrangle with her, Boyet, and she strikes at the brow.

BOYET: But she herself is hit lower: have I hit her now?

ROSALINE: Shall I come upon thee with an old saying that was a man when King Pippen of France was a little boy, as touching the hit it?

BOYET: So I may answer thee with one as old that was a woman when Queen Guinevere of Britain was a little wench, as touching the hit it.

ROSALINE: Thou canst not hit it, hit it, hit it,
   Thou canst not hit it, my good man.

BOYET: An I cannot, cannot, cannot,
   An I cannot, another can.

Exit ROSALINE

COSTARD: By my troth, most pleasant, how both did fit it!

MARIA: A mark marvellous well shot, for they both did hit it.

BOYET: A mark, O mark but that mark! A mark, says my lady. Let the mark have a prick in't to mete at, if it may be.

MARIA: Wide o'the bow hand, i'faith your hand is out.

COSTARD: Indeed he must shoot nearer, or he'll ne'er hit the clout.

BOYET: An if my hand be out, then belike your hand is in.

COSTARD: Then will she get the upshoot by cleaving the pin.

MARIA: Come come, you talk greasily, your lips grow foul.

COSTARD: She's too hard for you at pricks, sir, challenge her to bowl.

BOYET: I fear too much rubbing. Goodnight my good owl.

Exeunt all but COSTARD

COSTARD: By my soul, a swain, a most simple clown.
    Lord Lord, how the ladies and I have put him down!
    O'my troth, most sweet jests, most incony vulgar wit,
    When it comes so smoothly off, so obscenely, as it were, so fit!
    Armado o'th' t'other side, O a most dainty man,
    To see him walk before a lady and to bear her fan,
    To see him kiss his hand, and how most sweetly he will swear,
    And his page o' t'other side, that handful of wit:
    Ah heavens, it is a most pathetical nit!

Shot within

Sola, sola!

                                           Exit

SCENE SIX

Enter DULL, HOLOFERNES the pedant, and NATHANIEL the curate

NATHANIEL: Very reverend sport truly, and done in the testimony of a good conscience.

HOLOFERNES: The deer was, as you know, *sanguis*, in blood, ripe as the pomewater who now hangeth like a jewel in the ear of *caelum*, the sky, the welkin, the heaven, and anon falleth like a crab on the face of *terra*, the soil, the land, the earth.

NATHANIEL: Truly Master Holofernes, the epithets are sweetly varied, like a scholar at the least; but sir, I assure ye it was a buck of the first head.

HOLOFERNES: Sir Nathaniel, *haud credo*.

DULL: 'Twas not a auld grey doe, 'twas a pricket.

HOLOFERNES: Most barbarous intimation! Yet a kind of insinuation, as it were *in via*, in way, of explication, *facere*, as it were, replication, or rather *ostentare*, to show, as it were, his inclination after his undressed, unpolished, uneducated, unpruned, untrained, or rather unlettered, or ratherest unconfirmed fashion, to insert again my *haud credo* for a deer.

DULL: I said the deer was not a auld grey doe, 'twas a pricket.

HOLOFERNES: Twice-sod simplicity, *bis coctus*!
O thou monster ignorance, how deformèd dost thou look!

NATHANIEL: Sir, he hath never fed of the dainties that are bred in a book.
He hath not eat paper, as it were, he hath not drunk ink.
His intellect is not replenished, he is only an animal, only sensible in the duller parts,
And such barren plants are set before us that we thankful should be,

Which we of taste and feeling are, for those parts that do
    fructify in us more than he.
For as it would ill become me to be vain, indiscreet, or a fool,
So were there a patch set on learning to see him in a school.
But *omne bene* say I, being of an old father's mind:
Many can brook the weather that love not the wind.

DULL: You two are bookmen. Can you tell me by your wit
    What was a month old at Cain's birth that's not five weeks old
    as yet?

HOLOFERNES: *Dictynna* Goodman Dull, *Dictynna* Goodman
    Dull.

DULL: What is '*Dictima*'?

NATHANIEL: A title to Phoebe, to *luna*, to the moon.

HOLOFERNES: The moon was a month old when Adam was no
    more,
    And raught not to five weeks when he came to five score.
    Th'allusion holds in the exchange.

DULL: 'Tis true indeed, the collusion holds in the exchange.

HOLOFERNES: God comfort thy capacity, I say th'allusion
    holds in the exchange.

DULL: And I say the pollution holds in the exchange; for the
    moon is never but a month old; and I say beside that 'twas
    a pricket that the Princess killed.

HOLOFERNES: Sir Nathaniel, will you hear an extemporal
    epitaph on the death of the deer? And to humour the
    ignorant call I the deer the Princess killed a pricket.

NATHANIEL: *Perge*, good Master Holofernes, *perge*, so it shall
    please you to abrogate scurrility.

HOLOFERNES: I will something affect the letter, for it argues
    facility:
    The preyful Princess pierced and pricked a pretty pleasing
    pricket.

> Some say a sore, but not a sore till now made sore with
>   shooting.
> The dogs did yell; put 'L' to 'sore', then sorel jumps from
>   thicket,
> Or pricket sore, or else sorel; the people fall a-hooting.
> If sore be sore, then 'L' to sore makes fifty sores, o' sorel:
> Of one sore I an hundred make by adding but one more 'L'.

NATHANIEL: A rare talent!

DULL: If a talent be a claw, look how he claws him with a talent.

HOLOFERNES: This is a gift that I have, simple, simple: a foolish extravagant spirit, full of forms, figures, shapes, objects, ideas, apprehensions, motions, revolutions. These are begot in the ventricle of memory, nourished in the womb of *pia mater*, and delivered upon the mellowing of occasion; but the gift is good in those in whom it is acute, and I am thankful for it.

NATHANIEL: Sir, I praise the Lord for you, and so may my parishioners; for their sons are well tutored by you, and their daughters profit very greatly under you. You are a good member of the commonwealth.

HOLOFERNES: *Mehercle*, if their sons be ingenious they shall want no instruction; if their daughters be capable, I will put it to them. But *Vir sapit qui pauca loquitur*, a soul feminine saluteth us.

Enter JAQUENETTA and COSTARD the clown

JAQUENETTA: God give you good morrow, Master Parson.

HOLOFERNES: Master Parson, *quasi* 'pierce one'? And if one should be pierced, which is the one?

COSTARD: Marry Master Schoolmaster, he that is likest to a hogshead.

HOLOFERNES: 'Of piercing a hogshead': a good lustre of
conceit in a turf of earth, fire enough for a flint, pearl
enough for a swine: 'tis pretty, it is well.

JAQUENETTA: Good Master Parson, be so good as read me
this letter. It was given me by Costard, and sent me from
Don Armado. I beseech you read it.

HOLOFERNES: '*Fauste precor gelida quando pecus omne sub umbra
ruminat*', and so forth. Ah good old Mantuan, I may speak
of thee as the traveller doth of Venice:
> *Venezia, Venezia,*
> *Chi non ti vede, non ti prezia.*

Old Mantuan, old Mantuan, who understandeth thee not,
loves thee not. Ut re sol la mi fa. – Under pardon sir, what
are the contents? Or rather, as Horace says in his – what
my soul, verses?

NATHANIEL: Ay sir, and very learnèd.

HOLOFERNES: Let me hear a staff, a stanza, a verse. *Lege,
domine.*

NATHANIEL: 'If love make me forsworn, how shall I swear to
love?
Ah never faith could hold, if not to beauty vowed.
Though to myself forsworn, to thee I'll faithful prove.
Those thoughts to me were oaks, to thee like osiers bowed.
Study his bias leaves, and makes his book thine eyes,
Where all those pleasures live that art would comprehend.
If knowledge be the mark, to know thee shall suffice.
Well learnèd is that tongue that well can thee commend;
All ignorant that soul that sees thee without wonder;
Which is to me some praise that I thy parts admire.
Thine eye Jove's lightning bears, thy voice his dreadful
thunder,
Which not to anger bent, is music and sweet fire.
Celestial as thou art, O pardon, love, this wrong,
That sings heaven's praise with such an earthly tongue.'

HOLOFERNES: You find not the apostrophas, and so miss the accent. Let me supervise the canzonet. Here are only numbers ratified; but for the elegancy, facility, and golden cadence of poesy, *caret*; Ovidius Naso was the man. And why indeed 'Naso' but for smelling out the odoriferous flowers of fancy, the jerks of invention? *Imitari* is nothing: so doth the hound his master, the ape his keeper, the tired horse his rider. But damosella virgin, was this directed to you?

JAQUENETTA: Ay sir.

HOLOFERNES: I will overglance the superscript. 'To the snow-white hand of the most beauteous Lady Rosaline.' I will look again on the intellect of the letter, for the nomination of the party writing to the person written unto. 'Your ladyship's in all desired employment, Berowne.' Sir Nathaniel, this Berowne is one of the votaries with the King, and here he hath framed a letter to a sequent of the stranger Queen's, which accidentally, or by the way of progression, hath miscarried. – Trip and go, my sweet, deliver this paper into the royal hand of the King, it may concern much. Stay not thy compliment, I forgive thy duty, adieu.

JAQUENETTA: Good Costard, go with me. – Sir, God save your life.

COSTARD: Have with thee, my girl.

Exit with JAQUENETTA

NATHANIEL: Sir, you have done this in the fear of God very religiously, and as a certain father saith –

HOLOFERNES: Sir, tell not me of the father, I do fear colourable colours. But to return to the verses, did they please you, Sir Nathaniel?

NATHANIEL: Marvellous well for the pen.

HOLOFERNES: I do dine today at the father's of a certain pupil of mine, where if before repast it shall please you to gratify the table with a grace, I will on my privilege I have with the parents of the foresaid child or pupil undertake your *ben venuto*, where I will prove those verses to be very unlearnèd, neither savouring of poetry, wit, nor invention. I beseech your society.

NATHANIEL: And thank you too, for society, saith the text, is the happiness of life.

HOLOFERNES: And certes, the text most infallibly concludes it. (*To DULL*) Sir, I do invite you too. You shall not say me nay, *pauca verba*. Away, the gentles are at their game, and we will to our recreation.

Exeunt

SCENE SEVEN

Enter BEROWNE with a paper in his hand, alone

BEROWNE: 'The King he is hunting the deer, I am coursing
    myself.
    They have pitched a toil, I am toiling in a pitch,
    Pitch that defiles –'
    Defile, a foul word. Well, set thee down sorrow; for so they
    say the fool said, and so say I, and I the fool: well proved
    wit. By the Lord, this love is as mad as Ajax, it kills sheep,
    it kills me, I a sheep: well proved again o'my side. I will
    not love. If I do, hang me; i'faith I will not. O but her eye!
    By this light, but for her eye I would not love her. Yes, for
    her two eyes. Well, I do nothing in the world but lie, and
    lie in my throat. By heaven, I do love, and it hath taught
    me to rhyme and to be melancholy, and here is part of my
    rhyme, and here my melancholy. Well, she hath one o' my
    sonnets already. The clown bore it, the fool sent it, and the
    lady hath it: sweet clown, sweeter fool, sweetest lady. By
    the world, I would not care a pin if the other three were
    in. Here comes one with a paper, God give him grace to
    groan.

He stands aside. The KING entereth

KING: Ay me!

BEROWNE: Shot, by heaven! Proceed sweet Cupid, thou hast
    thumped him with thy birdbolt under the left pap. In faith,
    secrets.

KING: (*Reads*) 'So sweet a kiss the golden sun gives not
    To those fresh morning drops upon the rose
    As thy eyebeams when their fresh rays have smote
    The night of dew that on my cheeks down flows.
    Nor shines the silver moon one half so bright
    Through the transparent bosom of the deep
    As doth thy face through tears of mine give light.
    Thou shin'st in every tear that I do weep,
    No drop but as a coach doth carry thee,

So ridest thou triumphing in my woe.
Do but behold the tears that swell in me
And they thy glory through my grief will show.
But do not love thyself, then thou wilt keep
My tears for glasses, and still make me weep.
O Queen of queens, how far dost thou excel,
No thought can think nor tongue of mortal tell.'
How shall she know my griefs? I'll drop the paper.
Sweet leaves, shade folly. Who is he comes here?

Enter LONGAVILLE. The KING steps aside

What, Longaville, and reading; listen ear!

BEROWNE: Now in thy likeness one more fool appear!

LONGAVILLE: Ay me, I am forsworn.

BEROWNE: Why he comes in like a perjure, wearing papers.

KING: In love I hope, sweet fellowship in shame.

BEROWNE: One drunkard loves another of the name.

LONGAVILLE: Am I the first that have been perjured so?

BEROWNE: I could put thee in comfort, not by two that I know.
Thou makest the triumviry, the corner-cap of society,
The shape of love's Tyburn, that hangs up simplicity.

LONGAVILLE: I fear these stubborn lines lack power to move.
'O sweet Maria, empress of my love' –
These numbers will I tear, and write in prose.

BEROWNE: O rhymes are guards on wanton Cupid's hose,
Disfigure not his shop.

LONGAVILLE: This same shall go.

He reads the sonnet

'Did not the heavenly rhetoric of thine eye,
'Gainst whom the world cannot hold argument,
Persuade my heart to this false perjury?
Vows for thee broke deserve not punishment.

A woman I forswore, but I will prove,
Thou being a goddess, I forswore not thee.
My vow was earthly, thou a heavenly love.
Thy grace being gained cures all disgrace in me.
Vows are but breath, and breath a vapour is.
Then thou, fair sun, which on my earth dost shine,
Exhal'st this vapour-vow; in thee it is.
If broken then, it is no fault of mine;
If by me broke, what fool is not so wise
To lose an oath to win a paradise?'

BEROWNE: This is the liver vein, which makes flesh a deity,
A green goose a goddess, pure pure idolatry.
God amend us, God amend, we are much out o'th' way.

Enter DUMAINE

LONGAVILLE: By whom shall I send this? Company? Stay.

BEROWNE: All hid, all hid, an old infant play.
Like a demigod here sit I in the sky,
And wretched fools' secrets heedfully o'er-eye.
More sacks to the mill! O heavens, I have my wish.
Dumaine transformed: four woodcocks in a dish!

DUMAINE: O most divine Kate!

BEROWNE: O most profane coxcomb!

DUMAINE: By heaven, the wonder in a mortal eye!

BEROWNE: By earth, she is not, corporal, there you lie.

DUMAINE: Her amber hairs for foul hath amber quoted.

BEROWNE: An amber-coloured raven was well noted.

DUMAINE: As upright as the cedar.

BEROWNE: Stoop I say,
Her shoulder is with child.

DUMAINE: As fair as day.

BEROWNE: Ay, as some days, but then no sun must shine.

DUMAINE: O that I had my wish!

LONGAVILLE: And I had mine!

KING: And mine too, good Lord!

BEROWNE: Amen, so I had mine: is not that a good word?

DUMAINE: I would forget her, but a fever she
    Reigns in my blood and will remembered be.

BEROWNE: A fever in your blood, why then incision
    Would let her out in saucers: sweet misprision.

DUMAINE: Once more I'll read the ode that I have writ.

BEROWNE: Once more I'll mark how love can vary wit.

    DUMAINE reads his sonnet

DUMAINE: 'On a day, alack the day,
      Love, whose month is ever May,
      Spied a blossom passing fair
      Playing in the wanton air.
      Through the velvet leaves the wind
      All unseen can passage find,
      That the lover, sick to death,
      Wished himself the heavens' breath.
      "Air", quoth he, "thy cheeks may blow;
      Air, would I might triumph so.
      But alack, my hand is sworn
      Ne'er to pluck thee from thy thorn:
      Vow alack for youth unmeet,
      Youth so apt to pluck a sweet.
      Do not call it sin in me
      That I am forsworn for thee,
      Thou for whom great Jove would swear
      Juno but an Ethiop were,
      And deny himself for Jove,
      Turning mortal for thy love."'
    This will I send, and something else more plain,
    That shall express my true love's fasting pain.

O would the King, Berowne, and Longaville
Were lovers too; ill to example ill
Would from my forehead wipe a perjured note,
For none offend where all alike do dote.

LONGAVILLE: Dumaine, thy love is far from charity,
That in love's grief desir'st society.
You may look pale, but I should blush I know,
To be o'erheard and taken napping so.

KING: Come sir, you blush; as his, your case is such.
You chide at him, offending twice as much.
You do not love Maria? Longaville
Did never sonnet for her sake compile,
Nor never lay his wreathèd arms athwart
His loving bosom to keep down his heart?
I have been closely shrouded in this bush,
And marked you both, and for you both did blush.
I heard your guilty rhymes, observed your fashion,
Saw sighs reek from you, noted well your passion.
'Ay me!' says one, 'O Jove!' the other cries.
One, her hairs were gold; crystal the other's eyes.
(*To LONGAVILLE*) You would for paradise break faith and troth,
(*To DUMAINE*) And Jove for your love would infringe an oath.
What will Berowne say when that he shall hear
Faith so infringèd, which such zeal did swear?
How will he scorn, how will he spend his wit,
How will he triumph, leap, and laugh at it!
For all the wealth that ever I did see
I would not have him know so much by me.

BEROWNE: Now step I forth to whip hypocrisy.
Ah good my liege, I pray thee pardon me.
Good heart, what grace hast thou thus to reprove
These worms for loving, that art most in love?
Your eyes do make no coaches; in your tears
There is no certain princess that appears.
You'll not be perjured, 'tis a hateful thing;
Tush, none but minstrels like of sonneting.
But are you not ashamed, nay are you not,

All three of you, to be thus much o'ershot?
You found his mote, the King your mote did see,
But I a beam do find in each of three.
O what a scene of fool'ry have I seen,
Of sighs, of groans, of sorrow, and of teen!
O me, with what strict patience have I sat,
To see a king transformèd to a gnat!
To see great Hercules whipping a gig,
And profound Solomon to tune a jig,
And Nestor play at pushpin with the boys,
And critic Timon laugh at idle toys.
Where lies thy grief, O tell me good Dumaine?
And gentle Longaville, where lies thy pain?
And where my liege's? All about the breast.
A caudle ho!

KING: Too bitter is thy jest.
Are we betrayed thus to thy over-view?

BEROWNE: Not you to me, but I betrayed by you.
I that am honest, I that hold it sin
To break the vow I am engagèd in.
I am betrayed by keeping company
With men like you, men of inconstancy.
When shall you see me write a thing in rhyme,
Or groan for Joan, or spend a minute's time
In pruning me? When shall you hear that I
Will praise a hand, a foot, a face, an eye,
A gait, a state, a brow, a breast, a waist,
A leg, a limb?

KING: Soft, whither away so fast?
A true man or a thief, that gallops so?

BEROWNE: I post from love; good lover, let me go.

Enter JAQUENETTA and COSTARD the clown

JAQUENETTA: God bless the King!

KING: What present hast thou there?

COSTARD: Some certain treason.

KING: What makes treason here?

COSTARD: Nay, it makes nothing, sir.

KING: If it mar nothing neither,
The treason and you go in peace away together.

JAQUENETTA: I beseech your grace, let this letter be read.
Our parson misdoubts it; 'twas treason, he said.

KING: Berowne, read it over.

BEROWNE reads the letter

Where hadst thou it?

JAQUENETTA: Of Costard.

KING: Where hadst thou it?

COSTARD: Of Dun Adramadio, Dun Adramadio.

KING: How now, what is in you, why dost thou tear it?

BEROWNE: A toy, my liege, a toy, your grace needs not fear it.

LONGAVILLE: It did move him to passion, and therefore let's
hear it.

DUMAINE: It is Berowne's writing, and here is his name.

BEROWNE: (*To COSTARD*) Ah you whoreson loggerhead, you
were born to do me shame!
Guilty my lord, guilty, I confess, I confess.

KING: What?

BEROWNE: That you three fools lacked me fool to make up the
mess.
He, he, and you – and you, my liege – and I
Are pickpurses in love, and we deserve to die.
O dismiss this audience, and I shall tell you more.

DUMAINE: Now the number is even.

BEROWNE: True true, we are four.
 Will these turtles be gone?

KING: Hence sirs, away.

COSTARD: Walk aside the true folk, and let the traitors stay.
     Exeunt COSTARD and JAQUENETTA

BEROWNE: Sweet lords, sweet lovers, O let us embrace.
 As true we are as flesh and blood can be.
 The sea will ebb and flow, heaven show his face;
 Young blood doth not obey an old decree.
 We cannot cross the cause why we were born,
 Therefore of all hands must we be forsworn.

KING: What, did these rent lines show some love of thine?

BEROWNE: Did they, quoth you? Who sees the heavenly
   Rosaline
 But like a rude and savage man of Ind
 At the first op'ning of the gorgeous east,
 Bows not his vassal head and strucken blind,
 Kisses the base ground with obedient breast?
 What peremptory eagle-sighted eye
 Dares look upon the heaven of her brow
 That is not blinded by her majesty?

KING: What zeal, what fury hath inspired thee now?
 My love her mistress is a gracious moon,
 She an attending star, scarce seen a light.

BEROWNE: My eyes are then no eyes, nor I Berowne.
 O but for my love, day would turn to night.
 Of all complexions the culled sovereignty
 Do meet as at a fair in her fair cheek,
 Where several worthies make one dignity,
 Where nothing wants that want itself doth seek.
 Lend me the flourish of all gentle tongues –
 Fie painted rhetoric, O she needs it not.
 To things of sale a seller's praise belongs;
 She passes praise, then praise too short doth blot.
 A withered hermit fivescore winters worn

Might shake off fifty, looking in her eye.
Beauty doth varnish age as if new-born,
And gives the crutch the cradle's infancy.
O 'tis the sun that maketh all things shine.

KING: By heaven, thy love is black as ebony.

BEROWNE: Is ebony like her? O wood divine!
A wife of such wood were felicity.
O who can give an oath? Where is a book,
That I may swear beauty doth beauty lack
If that she learn not of her eye to look?
No face is fair that is not full so black.

KING: O paradox, black is the badge of hell,
The hue of dungeons and the school of night,
And beauty's crest becomes the heavens well.

BEROWNE: Devils soonest tempt, resembling spirits of light.
O if in black my lady's brows be decked,
It mourns that painting and usurping hair
Should ravish doters with a false aspect,
And therefore is she born to make black fair.
Her favour turns the fashion of the days,
For native blood is counted painting now,
And therefore red that would avoid dispraise
Paints itself black to imitate her brow.

DUMAINE: To look like her are chimney-sweepers black.

LONGAVILLE: And since her time are colliers counted bright.

KING: And Ethiops of their sweet complexion crack.

DUMAINE: Dark needs no candles now, for dark is light.

BEROWNE: Your mistresses dare never come in rain,
For fear their colours should be washed away.

KING: 'Twere good yours did, for sir, to tell you plain,
I'll find a fairer face not washed today.

BEROWNE: I'll prove her fair, or talk till doomsday here.

KING: No devil will fright thee then so much as she.

DUMAINE: I never knew man hold vile stuff so dear.

LONGAVILLE: Look, here's thy love, my foot and her face see.

BEROWNE: O if the streets were pavèd with thine eyes
    Her feet were much too dainty for such tread.

DUMAINE: O vile, then as she goes, what upward lies
    The street should see as she walked overhead.

KING: But what of this, are we not all in love?

BEROWNE: Nothing so sure, and thereby all forsworn.

KING: Then leave this chat, and good Berowne, now prove
    Our loving lawful and our faith not torn.

DUMAINE: Ay marry there, some flattery for this evil.

LONGAVILLE: O some authority how to proceed,
    Some tricks, some quillets how to cheat the devil.

DUMAINE: Some salve for perjury.

BEROWNE: O 'tis more than need.
    Have at you then, affection's men-at-arms.
    Consider what you first did swear unto:
    To fast, to study, and to see no woman:
    Flat treason 'gainst the kingly state of youth.
    Say, can you fast? Your stomachs are too young,
    And abstinence engenders maladies.
    O we have made a vow to study, lords,
    And in that vow we have forsworn our books;
    For when would you my liege, or you, or you,
    In leaden contemplation have found out
    Such fiery numbers as the prompting eyes
    Of beauty's tutors have enriched you with?
    Other slow arts entirely keep the brain,
    And therefore finding barren practisers,
    Scarce show a harvest of their heavy toil;
    But love, first learnèd in a lady's eyes,

Lives not alone immurèd in the brain,
But with the motion of all elements,
Courses as swift as thought in every power,
And gives to every power a double power,
Above their functions and their offices.
It adds a precious seeing to the eye:
A lover's eyes will gaze an eagle blind.
A lover's ear will hear the lowest sound
When the suspicious heed of theft is stopped.
Love's feeling is more soft and sensible
Than are the tender horns of cockled snails.
Love's tongue proves dainty Bacchus gross in taste.
For valour, is not love a Hercules,
Still climbing trees in the Hesperides,
Subtle as Sphinx, as sweet and musical
As bright Apollo's lute strung with his hair;
And when love speaks, the voice of all the gods
Make heaven drowsy with the harmony.
Never durst poet touch a pen to write
Until his ink were tempered with love's sighs.
O then his lines would ravish savage ears,
And plant in tyrants mild humility.
From women's eyes this doctrine I derive:
They sparkle still the right Promethean fire,
They are the books, the arts, the academes
That show, contain, and nourish all the world,
Else none at all in aught proves excellent.
Then fools you were these women to forswear,
Or keeping what is sworn, you will prove fools.
For wisdom's sake, a word that all men love,
Or for love's sake, a word that loves all men,
Or for men's sake, the authors of these women,
Or women's sake, by whom we men are men,
Let us once lose our oaths to find ourselves,
Or else we lose ourselves to keep our oaths.
It is religion to be thus forsworn,
For charity itself fulfils the law,
And who can sever love from charity?

KING: Saint Cupid then, and soldiers, to the field!

BEROWNE: Advance your standards, and upon them, lords.
Pell mell, down with them, but be first advised
In conflict that you get the sun of them.

LONGAVILLE: Now to plain dealing, lay these glozes by.
Shall we resolve to woo these girls of France?

KING: And win them too, therefore let us devise
Some entertainment for them in their tents.

BEROWNE: First from the park let us conduct them thither,
Then homeward every man attach the hand
Of his fair mistress; in the afternoon
We will with some strange pastime solace them,
Such as the shortness of the time can shape,
For revels, dances, masques, and merry hours
Forerun fair love, strewing her way with flowers.

KING: Away, away, no time shall be omitted
That will be time, and may by us be fitted.

BEROWNE: *Allons, allons*! Sowed cockle reaped no corn,
And justice always whirls in equal measure.
Light wenches may prove plagues to men forsworn;
If so, our copper buys no better treasure.

Exeunt

SCENE EIGHT

Enter HOLOFERNES the pedant, NATHANIEL the curate, and DULL

HOLOFERNES: *Satis quod sufficit.*

NATHANIEL: I praise God for you sir, your reasons at dinner have been sharp and sententious, pleasant without scurrility, witty without affectation, audacious without impudency, learnèd without opinion, and strange without heresy. I did converse this *quondam* day with a companion of the King's who is intituled, nominated, or called Don Adriano de Armado.

HOLOFERNES: *Novi hominem tanquam te.* His humour is lofty, his discourse peremptory, his tongue filed, his eye ambitious, his gait majestical, and his general behaviour vain, ridiculous, and thrasonical. He is too picked, too spruce, too affected, too odd, as it were, too peregrinate, as I may call it.

NATHANIEL: A most singular and choice epithet.

He draws out his table-book

HOLOFERNES: He draweth out the thread of his verbosity finer than the staple of his argument. I abhor such fanatical phantasims, such insociable and point-device companions, such rackers of orthography, as to speak 'dout', *sine* 'b', when he should say 'doubt'; 'det' when he should pronounce 'debt' – 'd, e, b, t', not 'd, e, t'. He clepeth a calf 'cauf', half 'hauf', neighbour *vocatur* 'nebour': 'neigh' abbreviated 'ne'. This is abhominable – which he would call 'abbominable'. It insinuateth me of *insanire – ne intelligis, domine?* – to make frantic, lunatic.

NATHANIEL: *Laus deo, bone intelligo.*

HOLOFERNES: *Bone? 'Bone'* for '*bene*': Priscian a little scratched; 'twill serve.

*Enter ARMADO the braggart, MOTH his boy, and COSTARD
the clown*

NATHANIEL: *Videsne quis venit?*

HOLOFERNES: *Video, et gaudeo.*

ARMADO: Chirrah.

HOLOFERNES: *Quare* 'chirrah', not 'sirrah'?

ARMADO: Men of peace, well encountered.

HOLOFERNES: Most military sir, salutation.

MOTH: They have been at a great feast of languages and stolen
the scraps.

COSTARD: O they have lived long on the alms-basket
of words. I marvel thy master hath not eaten thee
for a word, for thou art not so long by the head as
honorificabilitudinitatibus. Thou art easier swallowed than a
flapdragon.

MOTH: Peace, the peal begins.

ARMADO: Monsieur, are you not lettered?

MOTH: Yes, yes, he teaches boys the horn-book. What is 'a, b'
spelled backward, with the horn on his head?

HOLOFERNES: Ba, *pueritia*, with a horn added.

MOTH: Ba, most silly sheep, with a horn! You hear his
learning.

HOLOFERNES: *Quis, quis*, thou consonant?

MOTH: The last of the five vowels if you repeat them, or the
fifth if I.

HOLOFERNES: I will repeat them: a, e, i –

MOTH: The sheep. The other two concludes it: o, u.

ARMADO: Now by the salt wave of the *Mediterraneum* a sweet touch, a quick venue of wit: snip snap, quick and home. It rejoiceth my intellect: true wit.

MOTH: Offered by a child to an old man, which is 'wit-old'.

HOLOFERNES: What is the figure? What is the figure?

MOTH: Horns.

HOLOFERNES: Thou disputes like an infant. Go whip thy gig.

MOTH: Lend me your horn to make one, and I will whip about your infamy *manu cita*: – a gig of a cuckold's horn.

COSTARD: An I had but one penny in the world, thou shouldst have it to buy gingerbread. Hold, there is the very remuneration I had of thy master, thou halfpenny purse of wit, thou pigeon-egg of discretion. O an the heavens were so pleased that thou wert but my bastard, what a joyful father wouldst thou make me! Go to, thou hast it *ad dunghill*, at the fingers' ends, as they say.

HOLOFERNES: O I smell false Latin: 'dunghill' for *unguem*.

ARMADO: Arts-man, *perambulate*, we will be singled from the barbarous. Do you not educate youth at the charge-house on the top of the mountain?

HOLOFERNES: Or *mons*, the hill.

ARMADO: At your sweet pleasure, for the mountain.

HOLOFERNES: I do, sans question.

ARMADO: Sir, it is the King's most sweet pleasure and affection to congratulate the Princess at her pavilion in the posteriors of this day, which the rude multitude call the afternoon.

HOLOFERNES: The posterior of the day, most generous sir, is liable, congruent, and measurable for the afternoon. The word is well culled, choice, sweet, and apt, I do assure you sir, I do assure.

ARMADO: Sir, the King is a noble gentleman, and my familiar,
I do assure ye, very good friend: for what is inward
between us, let it pass. I do beseech thee, remember thy
courtesy, I beseech thee apparel thy head. And among
other important and most serious designs, and of great
import indeed too – but let that pass, for I must tell thee it
will please his grace, by the world, sometime to lean upon
my poor shoulder and with his royal finger thus dally with
my excrement, with my mustachio; but sweetheart, let that
pass. By the world, I recount no fable: some certain special
honours it pleaseth his greatness to impart to Armado, a
soldier, a man of travel, that hath seen the world – but
let that pass. The very all of all is – but sweetheart, I do
implore secrecy – that the King would have me present the
Princess, sweet chuck, with some delightful ostentation, or
show, or pageant, or antic, or firework. Now understanding
that the curate and your sweet self are good at such
eruptions and sudden breaking-out of mirth, as it were,
I have acquainted you withal to the end to crave your
assistance.

HOLOFERNES: Sir, you shall present before her the Nine
Worthies. Sir Nathaniel, as concerning some entertainment
of time, some show in the posterior of this day to be
rendered by our assistance, the King's command, and this
most gallant, illustrate, and learned gentleman, before the
Princess, I say none so fit as to present the Nine Worthies.

NATHANIEL: Where will you find men worthy enough to
present them?

HOLOFERNES: Joshua, yourself; myself, or this gallant
gentleman, Judas Maccabeus; this swain, because of his
great limb or joint, shall pass Pompey the Great; the page,
Hercules.

ARMADO: Pardon, sir, error: he is not quantity enough for that
Worthy's thumb, he is not so big as the end of his club.

91

HOLOFERNES: Shall I have audience? He shall present Hercules in minority: his enter and exit shall be strangling a snake, and I will have an apology for that purpose.

MOTH: An excellent device, so if any of the audience hiss, you may cry 'Well done, Hercules, now thou crushest the snake!' That is the way to make an offence gracious, though few have the grace to do it.

ARMADO: For the rest of the Worthies?

HOLOFERNES: I will play three myself.

MOTH: Thrice worthy gentleman!

ARMADO: Shall I tell you a thing?

HOLOFERNES: We attend.

ARMADO: We will have, if this fadge not, an antic. I beseech you follow.

HOLOFERNES: *Via* goodman Dull, thou hast spoken no word all this while.

DULL: Nor understood none neither, sir.

HOLOFERNES: *Allons*, we will employ thee.

DULL: I'll make one in a dance or so, or I will play on the tabor to the Worthies, and let them dance the hay.

HOLOFERNES: Most dull, honest Dull! To our sport, away.

Exeunt

SCENE NINE

Enter the Ladies

PRINCESS: Sweet hearts, we shall be rich ere we depart,
    If fairings come thus plentifully in.
    A lady walled about with diamonds:
    Look you what I have from the loving King.

ROSALINE: Madam, came nothing else along with that?

PRINCESS: Nothing but this? yes, as much love in rhyme
    As would be crammed up in a sheet of paper
    Writ on both sides the leaf, margin and all,
    That he was fain to seal on Cupid's name.

ROSALINE: That was the way to make his godhead wax,
    For he hath been five thousand year a boy.

KATHERINE: Ay, and a shrewd unhappy gallows too.

ROSALINE: You'll ne'er be friends with him, he killed your sister.

KATHERINE: He made her melancholy, sad, and heavy,
    And so she died; had she been light like you,
    Of such a merry, nimble, stirring spirit,
    She might ha' been a grandam ere she died;
    And so may you, for a light heart lives long.

ROSALINE: What's your dark meaning, mouse, of this light word?

KATHERINE: A light condition in a beauty dark.

ROSALINE: We need more light to find your meaning out.

KATHERINE: You'll mar the light by taking it in snuff,
    Therefore I'll darkly end the argument.

ROSALINE: Look what you do, you do it still i'th' dark.

KATHERINE: So do not you, for you are a light wench.

ROSALINE: Indeed I weigh not you, and therefore light.

KATHERINE: You weigh me not, O that's you care not for me.

ROSALINE: Great reason, for past cure is still past care.

PRINCESS: Well bandied both, a set of wit well played.
    But Rosaline, you have a favour, too.
    Who sent it, and what is it?

ROSALINE: I would you knew.
    An if my face were but as fair as yours
    My favour were as great, be witness this.
    Nay, I have verses too, I thank Berowne,
    The numbers true, and were the numb'ring too,
    I were the fairest goddess on the ground.
    I am compared to twenty thousand fairs.
    O he hath drawn my picture in his letter.

PRINCESS: Anything like?

ROSALINE: Much in the letters, nothing in the praise.

PRINCESS: Beauteous as ink: a good conclusion.

KATHERINE: Fair as a text B in a copy-book.

ROSALINE: Ware pencils, ho! Let me not die your debtor,
    My red dominical, my golden letter.
    O that your face were not so full of O's!

PRINCESS: A pox of that jest, I beshrew all shrews.
    But Katherine, what was sent to you from fair Dumaine?

KATHERINE: Madam, this glove.

PRINCESS: Did he not send you twain?

KATHERINE: Yes madam; and moreover,
    Some thousand verses of a faithful lover,
    A huge translation of hypocrisy
    Vilely compiled, profound simplicity.

MARIA: This and these pearls to me sent Longaville.
    The letter is too long by half a mile.

PRINCESS: I think no less. Dost thou not wish in heart
    The chain were longer and the letter short?

MARIA: Ay, or I would these hands might never part.

PRINCESS: We are wise girls to mock our lovers so.

ROSALINE: They are worse fools to purchase mocking so.
　　That same Berowne I'll torture ere I go.
　　O that I knew he were but in by th' week,
　　How I would make him fawn, and beg, and seek,
　　And wait the season, and observe the times,
　　And spend his prodigal wits in bootless rhymes,
　　And shape his service wholly to my hests,
　　And make him proud to make me proud that jests!
　　So planet-like would I o'ersway his state,
　　That he should be my fool, and I his fate.

PRINCESS: None are so surely caught when they are catched
　　As wit turned fool: folly in wisdom hatched
　　Hath wisdom's warrant, and the help of school,
　　And wit's own grace, to grace a learnèd fool.

ROSALINE: The blood of youth burns not with such excess
　　As gravity's revolt to wantonness.

MARIA: Folly in fools bears not so strong a note
　　As fool'ry in the wise when wit doth dote,
　　Since all the power thereof it doth apply
　　To prove by wit, worth in simplicity.

　　Enter BOYET

PRINCESS: Here comes Boyet, and mirth is in his face.

BOYET: O I am stabbed with laughter, where's her grace?

PRINCESS: Thy news, Boyet?

BOYET:　　　　　　　　Prepare madam, prepare.
　　Arm, wenches, arm, encounters mounted are
　　Against your peace: love doth approach disguised,
　　Armèd in arguments, you'll be surprised.
　　Muster your wits, stand in your own defence,
　　Or hide your heads like cowards and fly hence.

PRINCESS: Saint Denis to Saint Cupid! What are they
    That charge their breath against us? Say, scout, say.

BOYET: Under the cool shade of a sycamore
    I thought to close mine eyes some half an hour
    When lo, to interrupt my purposed rest
    Toward that shade I might behold addressed
    The King and his companions; warily
    I stole into a neighbour thicket by
    And overheard what you shall overhear:
    That by and by disguised they will be here.
    Their herald is a pretty knavish page
    That well by heart hath conned his embassage.
    Action and accent did they teach him there:
    'Thus must thou speak, and thus thy body bear.'
    And ever and anon they made a doubt
    Presence majestical would put him out,
    'For', quoth the King, 'an angel shalt thou see,
    Yet fear not thou, but speak audaciously.'
    The boy replied 'An angel is not evil.
    I should have feared her had she been a devil.'
    With that all laughed and clapped him on the shoulder,
    Making the bold wag by their praises bolder.
    One rubbed his elbow thus, and fleered, and swore
    A better speech was never spoke before.
    Another with his finger and his thumb
    Cried '*Via*, we will do't, come what will come!'
    The third he capered and cried 'All goes well!'
    The fourth turned on the toe and down he fell.
    With that they all did tumble on the ground,
    With such a zealous laughter so profound,
    That in this spleen ridiculous appears,
    To check their folly, passion's solemn tears.

PRINCESS: But what, but what, come they to visit us?

BOYET: They do, they do, and are apparelled thus:
    Like Muscovites or Russians, as I guess.
    Their purpose is to parley, to court and dance,
    And every one his love-suit will advance

Unto his several mistress, which they'll know
By favours several which they did bestow.

PRINCESS: And will they so? The gallants shall be tasked,
For ladies, we will every one be masked,
And not a man of them shall have the grace,
Despite of suit, to see a lady's face.
Hold Rosaline, this favour thou shalt wear,
And then the King will court thee for his dear.
Hold, take thou this, my sweet, and give me thine,
So shall Berowne take me for Rosaline.
And change you favours too, so shall your loves
Woo contrary, deceived by these removes.

ROSALINE: Come on then, wear the favours most in sight.

KATHERINE: But in this changing what is your intent?

PRINCESS: The effect of my intent is to cross theirs:
They do it but in mockery merriment,
And mock for mock is only my intent.
Their several counsels they unbosom shall
To loves mistook, and so be mocked withal
Upon the next occasion that we meet
With visages displayed to talk and greet.

ROSALINE: But shall we dance if they desire us to't?

PRINCESS: No, to the death we will not move a foot,
Nor to their penned speech render we no grace,
But while 'tis spoke each turn away her face.

BOYET: Why that contempt will kill the speaker's heart,
And quite divorce his memory from his part.

PRINCESS: Therefore I do it, and I make no doubt
The rest will ne'er come in if he be out.
There's no such sport as sport by sport o'erthrown,
To make theirs ours, and ours none but our own.
So shall we stay, mocking intended game,
And they well mocked depart away with shame.

A trumpet sounds

BOYET: The trumpet sounds, be masked, the masquers come.

*Enter blackamoors with music; the boy MOTH with a speech;
the KING and his Lords disguised*

MOTH: All hail, the richest beauties on the earth!

BOYET: Beauties no richer than rich taffeta.

MOTH: A holy parcel of the fairest dames –

The Ladies turn their backs to him

That ever turned their – backs to mortal views.

BEROWNE: Their eyes, villain, their eyes.

MOTH: That ever turned their eyes to mortal views.
Out –

BOYET: True, out indeed.

MOTH: Out of your favours, heavenly spirits, vouchsafe
Not to behold –

BEROWNE: Once to behold, rogue!

MOTH: Once to behold with your sun-beamèd eyes –
With your sun-beamèd eyes –

BOYET: They will not answer to that epithet,
You were best call it daughter-beamèd eyes.

MOTH: They do not mark me, and that brings me out.

BEROWNE: Is this your perfectness? Be gone you rogue!
Exit MOTH

ROSALINE: (*as the PRINCESS*) What would these strangers?
Know their minds Boyet.
If they do speak our language, 'tis our will
That some plain man recount their purposes.
Know what they would.

BOYET: What would you with the Princess?

BEROWNE: Nothing but peace and gentle visitation.

ROSALINE: What would they, say they?

BOYET: Nothing but peace and gentle visitation.

ROSALINE: Why that they have, and bid them so be gone.

BOYET: She says you have it, and you may be gone.

KING: Say to her we have measured many miles
    To tread a measure with her on this grass.

BOYET: They say that they have measured many a mile
    To tread a measure with you on this grass.

ROSALINE: It is not so: ask them how many inches
    Is in one mile; if they have measured many,
    The measure then of one is easily told.

BOYET: If to come hither you have measured miles,
    And many miles, the Princess bids you tell
    How many inches doth fill up one mile.

BEROWNE: Tell her we measure them by weary steps.

BOYET: She hears herself.

ROSALINE: How many weary steps
    Of many weary miles you have o'ergone
    Are numbered in the travel of one mile?

BEROWNE: We number nothing that we spend for you.
    Our duty is so rich, so infinite,
    That we may do it still without account.
    Vouchsafe to show the sunshine of your face
    That we like savages may worship it.

ROSALINE: My face is but a moon, and clouded too.

KING: Blessèd are clouds to do as such clouds do.
    Vouchsafe bright moon, and these thy stars to shine,
    Those clouds removed, upon our watery eyne.

ROSALINE: O vain petitioner, beg a greater matter,
   Thou now requests but moonshine in the water.

KING: Then in our measure do but vouchsafe one change.
   Thou bid'st me beg, this begging is not strange.

ROSALINE: Play music then. Nay you must do it soon.
   Not yet? no dance, thus change I like the moon.

KING: Will you not dance? How come you thus estranged?

ROSALINE: You took the moon at full but now she's changed.

KING: Yet still she is the moon, and I the man.
   The music plays, vouchsafe some motion to it.

ROSALINE: Our ears vouchsafe it.

KING: But your legs should do it.

ROSALINE: Since you are strangers and come here by chance
   We'll not be nice, take hands, we will not dance.

KING: Why take we hands then?

ROSALINE: Only to part friends.
   Curtsy sweet hearts, and so the measure ends.

KING: More measure of this measure, be not nice.

ROSALINE: We can afford no more at such a price.

KING: Price you yourselves; what buys your company?

ROSALINE: Your absence only.

KING: That can never be.

ROSALINE: Then cannot we be bought, and so adieu,
   Twice to your visor, and half once to you.

KING: If you deny to dance, let's hold more chat.

ROSALINE: In private then.

KING: I am best pleased with that.

BEROWNE: (*To the PRINCESS*) White-handed mistress, one sweet
    word with thee.

PRINCESS: (*As ROSALINE*) Honey and milk and sugar, there is
    three.

BEROWNE: Nay then two treys, an if you grow so nice,
    Metheglin, wort, and malmsey, well run dice:
    There's half-a-dozen sweets.

PRINCESS: Seventh sweet, adieu.
    Since you can cog, I'll play no more with you.

BEROWNE: One word in secret.

PRINCESS: Let it not be sweet.

BEROWNE: Thou griev'st my gall.

PRINCESS: Gall, bitter!

BEROWNE: Therefore meet.

DUMAINE: (*To MARIA*) Will you vouchsafe with me to change a
    word?

MARIA: (*As KATHERINE*) Name it.

DUMAINE: Fair lady –

MARIA: Say you so? Fair lord:
    Take that for your 'fair lady'.

DUMAINE: Please it you,
    As much in private, and I'll bid adieu.

KATHERINE: (*As MARIA*) What, was your visor made without a
    tongue?

LONGAVILLE: I know the reason, lady, why you ask.

KATHERINE: O for your reason, quickly sir, I long.

LONGAVILLE: You have a double tongue within your mask,
    And will afford my speechless visor half.

KATHERINE: 'Veal', quoth the Dutchman: is not veal a calf?

LONGAVILLE: A calf, fair lady?

KATHERINE: No, a fair lord calf.

LONGAVILLE: Let's part the word.

KATHERINE: No, I'll not be your half.
  Take all and wean it, it may prove an ox.

LONGAVILLE: Look how you butt yourself in these sharp mocks!
  Will you give horns, chaste lady? Do not so.

KATHERINE: Then die a calf before your horns do grow.

LONGAVILLE: One word in private with you ere I die.

KATHERINE: Bleat softly then, the butcher hears you cry.

BOYET: The tongues of mocking wenches are as keen
  As is the razor's edge invisible,
  Cutting a smaller hair than may be seen,
  Above the sense of sense; so sensible
  Seemeth their conference; their conceits have wings
  Fleeter than arrows, bullets, wind, thought, swifter things.

ROSALINE: Not one word more my maids, break off, break off.

BEROWNE: By heaven, all dry-beaten with pure scoff!

KING: Farewell mad wenches, you have simple wits.
                    Exeunt the KING, Lords, and blackamoors

PRINCESS: Twenty adieus, my frozen Muscovites.
  Are these the breed of wits so wondered at?

BOYET: Tapers they are, with your sweet breaths puffed out.

ROSALINE: Well-liking wits they have, gross, gross, fat, fat.

PRINCESS: O poverty in wit, kingly-poor flout!
  Will they not, think you, hang themselves tonight,
  Or ever but in visors show their faces?
  This pert Berowne was out of count'nance quite.

ROSALINE: O they were all in lamentable cases.
    The King was weeping-ripe for a good word.

PRINCESS: Berowne did swear himself out of all suit.

MARIA: Dumaine was at my service, and his sword.
    No point, quoth I: my servant straight was mute.

KATHERINE: Lord Longaville said I came o'er his heart,
    And trow you what he called me?

PRINCESS: Qualm, perhaps.

KATHERINE: Yes, in good faith.

PRINCESS: Go, sickness as thou art.

ROSALINE: Well, better wits have worn plain statute-caps.
    But will you hear? The King is my love sworn.

PRINCESS: And quick Berowne hath plighted faith to me.

KATHERINE: And Longaville was for my service born.

MARIA: Dumaine is mine, as sure as bark on tree.

BOYET: Madam and pretty mistresses, give ear.
    Immediately they will again be here
    In their own shapes, for it can never be
    They will digest this harsh indignity.

PRINCESS: Will they return?

BOYET: They will, they will, God knows,
    And leap for joy, though they are lame with blows.
    Therefore change favours, and when they repair,
    Blow like sweet roses in this summer air.

PRINCESS: How blow, how blow? Speak to be understood.

BOYET: Fair ladies masked are roses in their bud;
    Dismasked, their damask sweet commixture shown,
    Are angels vailing clouds, or roses blown.

PRINCESS: Avaunt perplexity! What shall we do
    If they return in their own shapes to woo?

ROSALINE: Good madam, if by me you'll be advised,
    Let's mock them still, as well known as disguised.
    Let us complain to them what fools were here,
    Disguised like Muscovites in shapeless gear,
    And wonder what they were, and to what end
    Their shallow shows, and prologue vilely penned,
    And their rough carriage so ridiculous,
    Should be presented at our tent to us.

BOYET: Ladies withdraw, the gallants are at hand.

PRINCESS: Whip to our tents, as roes runs over land!
                                        Exeunt the Ladies

Enter the KING, BEROWNE, DUMAINE, and LONGAVILLE

KING: Fair sir, God save you, where's the Princess?

BOYET: Gone to her tent. Please it your majesty
    Command me any service to her thither?

KING: That she vouchsafe me audience for one word.

BOYET: I will, and so will she, I know, my lord.
                                        Exit

BEROWNE: This fellow pecks up wit as pigeons peas,
    And utters it again when God doth please.
    He is wit's pedlar, and retails his wares
    At wakes and wassails, meetings, markets, fairs.
    And we that sell by gross, the Lord doth know,
    Have not the grace to grace it with such show.
    This gallant pins the wenches on his sleeve;
    Had he been Adam, he had tempted Eve.
    He can carve too, and lisp, why this is he
    That kissed his hand away in courtesy.
    This is the ape of form, Monsieur the Nice,
    That when he plays at tables chides the dice
    In honourable terms; nay he can sing

A mean most meanly, and in ushering
Mend him who can; the ladies call him sweet.
The stairs as he treads on them kiss his feet.
This is the flower that smiles on everyone
To show his teeth as white as whale's bone,
And consciences that will not die in debt
Pay him the due of honey-tongued Boyet.

KING: A blister on his sweet tongue with my heart,
That put Armado's page out of his part!

Enter the Ladies and BOYET

BEROWNE: See where it comes. Behaviour, what wert thou
Till this madman showed thee, and what art thou now?

KING: All hail sweet madam, and fair time of day!

PRINCESS: Fair in all hail is foul, as I conceive.

KING: Construe my speeches better, if you may.

PRINCESS: Then wish me better, I will give you leave.

KING: We came to visit you, and purpose now
To lead you to our court, vouchsafe it then.

PRINCESS: This field shall hold me, and so hold your vow.
Nor God nor I delights in perjured men.

KING: Rebuke me not for that which you provoke.
The virtue of your eye must break my oath.

PRINCESS: You nickname virtue, vice you should have spoke,
For virtue's office never breaks men's troth.
Now by my maiden honour, yet as pure
As the unsullied lily, I protest,
A world of torments though I should endure,
I would not yield to be your house's guest,
So much I hate a breaking cause to be
Of heavenly oaths vowed with integrity.

KING: O you have lived in desolation here,
Unseen, unvisited, much to our shame.

PRINCESS: Not so my lord, it is not so, I swear.
　　We have had pastimes here, and pleasant game.
　　A mess of Russians left us but of late.

KING: How, madam? Russians?

PRINCESS:　　　　　　　　　Ay in truth, my lord.
　　Trim gallants, full of courtship and of state.

ROSALINE: Madam, speak true. It is not so, my lord.
　　My lady, to the manner of the days,
　　In courtesy gives undeserving praise.
　　We four indeed confronted were with four
　　In Russian habit, here they stayed an hour,
　　And talked apace, and in that hour, my lord,
　　They did not bless us with one happy word.
　　I dare not call them fools, but this I think:
　　When they are thirsty, fools would fain have drink.

BEROWNE: This jest is dry to me. Gentle sweet,
　　Your wits makes wise things foolish; when we greet,
　　With eyes' best seeing, heaven's fiery eye,
　　By light we lose light: your capacity
　　Is of that nature that to your huge store
　　Wise things seem foolish, and rich things but poor.

ROSALINE: This proves you wise and rich, for in my eye –

BEROWNE: I am a fool, and full of poverty.

ROSALINE: But that you take what doth to you belong
　　It were a fault to snatch words from my tongue.

BEROWNE: O I am yours, and all that I possess.

ROSALINE: All the fool mine!

BEROWNE:　　　　　　　　　I cannot give you less.

ROSALINE: Which of the visors was it that you wore?

BEROWNE: Where, when, what visor, why demand you this?

ROSALINE: There, then, that visor, that superfluous case,

That hid the worse and showed the better face.

KING: We were descried, they'll mock us now downright.

DUMAINE: Let us confess, and turn it to a jest.

PRINCESS: Amazed, my lord: why looks your highness sad?

ROSALINE: Help, hold his brows, he'll swoon: why look
    you pale?
Seasick I think, coming from Muscovy.

BEROWNE: Thus pour the stars down plagues for perjury.
Can any face of brass hold longer out?
Here stand I, lady, dart thy skill at me,
Bruise me with scorn, confound me with a flout,
Thrust thy sharp wit quite through my ignorance,
Cut me to pieces with thy keen conceit,
And I will wish thee nevermore to dance,
Nor nevermore in Russian habit wait.
O never will I trust to speeches penned,
Nor to the motion of a schoolboy's tongue,
Nor never come in visor to my friend,
Nor woo in rhyme like a blind harper's song.
Taffeta phrases, silken terms precise,
Three-piled hyperboles, spruce affectation,
Figures pedantical, these summer flies
Have blown me full of maggot ostentation.
I do forswear them, and I here protest,
By this white glove – how white the hand, God knows –
Henceforth my wooing mind shall be expressed
In russet yeas, and honest kersey noes.
And to begin, wench – so God help me, law!
My love to thee is sound, *sans* crack or flaw.

ROSALINE: Sans *sans*, I pray you.

BEROWNE: Yet I have a trick
Of the old rage; bear with me, I am sick.
I'll leave it by degrees. Soft, let us see.
Write 'Lord have mercy on us' on those three.
They are infected, in their hearts it lies.

They have the plague, and caught it of your eyes.
These lords are visited, you are not free;
For the Lord's tokens on you do I see.

PRINCESS: No, they are free that gave these tokens to us.

BEROWNE: Our states are forfeit, seek not to undo us.

ROSALINE: It is not so, for how can this be true,
That you stand forfeit, being those that sue?

BEROWNE: Peace, for I will not have to do with you.

ROSALINE: Nor shall not, if I do as I intend.

BEROWNE: Speak for yourselves, my wit is at an end.

KING: Teach us, sweet madam, for our rude transgression
Some fair excuse.

PRINCESS: The fairest is confession.
Were not you here but even now disguised?

KING: Madam, I was.

PRINCESS: And were you well advised?

KING: I was, fair madam.

PRINCESS: When you then were here,
What did you whisper in your lady's ear?

KING: That more than all the world I did respect her.

PRINCESS: When she shall challenge this, you will reject her.

KING: Upon mine honour, no.

PRINCESS: Peace, peace, forbear.
Your oath once broke, you force not to forswear.

KING: Despise me when I break this oath of mine.

PRINCESS: I will, and therefore keep it. Rosaline,
What did the Russian whisper in your ear?

ROSALINE: Madam, he swore that he did hold me dear

As precious eyesight, and did value me
Above this world, adding thereto moreover
That he would wed me, or else die my lover.

PRINCESS: God give thee joy of him! The noble lord
Most honourably doth uphold his word.

KING: What mean you, madam? By my life, my troth,
I never swore this lady such an oath.

ROSALINE: By heaven you did, and to confirm it plain,
You gave me this, but take it, sir, again.

KING: My faith and this the Princess I did give,
I knew her by this jewel on her sleeve.

PRINCESS: Pardon me, sir, this jewel did she wear,
And Lord Berowne, I thank him, is my dear.
What, will you have me, or your pearl again?

BEROWNE: Neither of either, I remit both twain.
I see the trick on't: here was a consent,
Knowing aforehand of our merriment,
To dash it like a Christmas comedy.
Some carry-tale, some please-man, some slight zany,
Some mumble-news, some trencher-knight, some Dick
That smiles his cheek in years, and knows the trick
To make my lady laugh when she's disposed,
Told our intents before, which once disclosed,
The ladies did change favours, and then we,
Following the signs, wooed but the sign of she.
Now to our perjury to add more terror,
We are again forsworn, in will and error.
Much upon this 'tis, (*To BOYET*) and might not you
Forestall our sport, to make us thus untrue?
Do not you know my lady's foot by th' square,
And laugh upon the apple of her eye,
And stand between her back, sir, and the fire,
Holding a trencher, jesting merrily?
You put our page out. Go, you are allowed.
Die when you will, a smock shall be your shroud.

You leer upon me, do you? There's an eye
Wounds like a leaden sword.

BOYET: Full merrily
Hath this brave manage, this career been run.

BEROWNE: Lo, he is tilting straight. Peace, I have done.

Enter COSTARD the clown

Welcome pure wit, thou partest a fair fray.

COSTARD: O Lord sir, they would know
Whether the three Worthies shall come in or no.

BEROWNE: What, are there but three?

COSTARD: No sir, but it is vara fine,
For everyone pursents three.

BEROWNE: And three times thrice is nine.

COSTARD: Not so sir, under correction sir, I hope it is not so.
You cannot beg us sir, I can assure you sir, we know what we
know.
I hope sir, three times thrice, sir –

BEROWNE: Is not nine?

COSTARD: Under correction sir, we know whereuntil it doth
amount.

BEROWNE: By Jove, I always took three threes for nine.

COSTARD: O Lord sir, it were pity you should get your living
by reck'ning, sir.

BEROWNE: How much is it?

COSTARD: O Lord sir, the parties themselves, the actors, sir,
will show whereuntil it doth amount. For mine own part, I
am, as they say, but to parfect one man in one poor man,
Pompion the Great, sir.

BEROWNE: Art thou one of the Worthies?

COSTARD: It pleased them to think me worthy of Pompey the
    Great. For mine own part, I know not the degree of the
    Worthy, but I am to stand for him.

BEROWNE: Go bid them prepare.

COSTARD: We will turn it finely off, sir, we will take some care.

                                            Exit

KING: Berowne, they will shame us, let them not approach.

BEROWNE: We are shame-proof, my lord, and 'tis some policy
    To have one show worse than the King's and his company.

KING: I say they shall not come.

PRINCESS: Nay my good lord, let me o'errule you now.
    That sport best pleases that doth least know how.
    Where zeal strives to content, and the contents
    Dies in the zeal of that which it presents,
    There form confounded makes most form in mirth,
    When great things labouring perish in their birth.

BEROWNE: A right description of our sport, my lord.

    Enter ARMADO the braggart

ARMADO: Anointed, I implore so much expense of thy royal
    sweet breath as will utter a brace of words.

PRINCESS: Doth this man serve God?

BEROWNE: Why ask you?

PRINCESS: He speaks not like a man of God his making.

ARMADO: That is all one, my fair sweet honey monarch, for I
    protest, the schoolmaster is exceeding fantastical, too-too
    vain, too-too vain; but we will put it, as they say, to *fortuna
    de la guerra.* I wish you the peace of mind, most royal
    couplement.

                                                Exit

KING: Here is like to be a good presence of Worthies. He
    presents Hector of Troy, the swain Pompey the Great, the

parish curate Alexander, Armado's page Hercules, the
pedant Judas Maccabeus;
And if these four Worthies in their first show thrive,
These four will change habits and present the other five.

BEROWNE: There is five in the first show.

KING: You are deceived, 'tis not so.

BEROWNE: The pedant, the braggart, the hedge-priest, the fool,
   and the boy,
Abate throw at novum and the whole world again
Cannot pick out five such, take each one in his vein.

KING: The ship is under sail, and here she comes amain.

Enter COSTARD as Pompey

COSTARD: I Pompey am –

BEROWNE: You lie, you are not he.

COSTARD: I Pompey am –

BOYET: With leopard's head on knee.

BEROWNE: Well said, old mocker, I must needs be friends
   with thee.

COSTARD: I Pompey am, Pompey surnamed the Big.

DUMAINE: 'The Great'.

COSTARD: It is 'Great', sir. Pompey surnamed the Great,
   That oft in field with targe and shield did make my foe
      to sweat,
   And travelling along this coast I here am come by chance,
   And lay my arms before the legs of this sweet lass of France.
   If your ladyship would say 'Thanks, Pompey', I had done.

PRINCESS: Great thanks, great Pompey.

COSTARD: 'Tis not so much worth, but I hope I was perfect. I
   made a little fault in 'great'.

BEROWNE: My hat to a halfpenny Pompey proves the best Worthy.

Enter NATHANIEL the curate as Alexander

NATHANIEL: When in the world I lived I was the world's commander.
By east, west, north, and south, I spread my conquering might.
My scutcheon plain declares that I am Alisander.

BOYET: Your nose says no, you are not, for it stands too right.

BEROWNE: Your nose smells 'no' in this, most tender-smelling knight.

PRINCESS: The conqueror is dismayed; proceed, good Alexander.

NATHANIEL: When in the world I lived I was the world's commander.

BOYET: Most true, 'tis right, you were so, Alisander.

BEROWNE: Pompey the Great.

COSTARD: Your servant, and Costard.

BEROWNE: Take away the conqueror, take away Alisander.

COSTARD: O sir, you have overthrown Alisander the Conqueror; you will be scraped out of the painted cloth for this. Your lion that holds his pole-axe sitting on a close-stool will be given to Ajax, he will be the ninth Worthy. A conqueror and afeard to speak? Run away for shame, Alisander.

Exit NATHANIEL

There, an't shall please you, a foolish mild man, an honest man, look you, and soon dashed. He is a marvellous good neighbour, faith, and a very good bowler, but for Alisander, alas you see how 'tis, a little o'erparted. But there are Worthies a-coming will speak their mind in some other sort.

PRINCESS: Stand aside, good Pompey.

Enter HOLOFERNES the pedant as Judas, and the boy MOTH as Hercules

HOLOFERNES: Great Hercules is presented by this imp,
　　Whose club killed Cerberus, that three-headed *canus*,
　　And when he was a babe, a child, a shrimp,
　　Thus did he strangle serpents in his *manus*.
　　Quoniam he seemeth in minority,
　　Ergo I come with this apology.
　　Keep some state in thy exit, and vanish.

MOTH retires

HOLOFERNES: Judas I am –

DUMAINE: A Judas?

HOLOFERNES: Not Iscariot, sir.
　　Judas I am, yclippèd Maccabeus.

DUMAINE: Judas Maccabeus clipped is plain Judas.

BEROWNE: A kissing traitor. How art thou proved Judas?

HOLOFERNES: Judas I am –

DUMAINE: The more shame for you Judas.

HOLOFERNES: What mean you sir?

BOYET: To make Judas hang himself.

HOLOFERNES: Begin sir, you are my elder.

BEROWNE: Well followed, Judas was hanged on an elder.

HOLOFERNES: I will not be put out of countenance.

BEROWNE: Because thou hast no face.

HOLOFERNES: What is this?

BOYET: A cittern-head.

DUMAINE: The head of a bodkin.

BEROWNE: A death's face in a ring.

LONGAVILLE: The face of an old Roman coin, scarce seen.

BOYET: The pommel of Caesar's falchion.

DUMAINE: The carved-bone face on a flask.

BEROWNE: Saint George's half-cheek in a brooch.

DUMAINE: Ay and in a brooch of lead.

BEROWNE: Ay and worn in the cap of a tooth-drawer. And now forward, for we have put thee in countenance.

HOLOFERNES: You have put me out of countenance.

BEROWNE: False, we have given thee faces.

HOLOFERNES: But you have outfaced them all.

BEROWNE: An thou wert a lion, we would do so.

BOYET: Therefore as he is an ass, let him go.
And so adieu sweet Jude. Nay, why dost thou stay?

DUMAINE: For the latter end of his name.

BEROWNE: For the ass to the Jude, give it him: Jud-as, away.

HOLOFERNES: This is not generous, not gentle, not humble.

BOYET: A light for Monsieur Judas, it grows dark, he may stumble.

Exit HOLOFERNES

PRINCESS: Alas poor Maccabeus, how hath he been baited!

Enter ARMADO the braggart as Hector

BEROWNE: Hide thy head Achilles, here comes Hector in arms.

DUMAINE: Though my mocks come home by me, I will now be merry.

KING: Hector was but a Trojan in respect of this.

BOYET: But is this Hector?

KING: I think Hector was not so clean-timbered.

LONGAVILLE: His leg is too big for Hector's.

DUMAINE: More calf, certain.

BOYET: No, he is best endowed in the small.

BEROWNE: This cannot be Hector.

DUMAINE: He's a god or a painter, for he makes faces.

ARMADO: The armipotent Mars, of lances the almighty,
　　Gave Hector a gift –

DUMAINE: A gilt nutmeg.

BEROWNE: A lemon.

LONGAVILLE: Stuck with cloves.

DUMAINE: No, cloven.

ARMADO: Peace!
　　The armipotent Mars, of lances the almighty,
　　Gave Hector a gift, the heir of Ilion,
　　A man so breathed that certain he would fight, yea,
　　From morn till night, out of his pavilion.
　　I am that flower –

DUMAINE:　　　　　　　　That mint.

LONGAVILLE:　　　　　　　　That colombine.

ARMADO: Sweet Lord Longaville, rein thy tongue.

LONGAVILLE: I must rather give it the rein, for it runs against
　　Hector.

DUMAINE: Ay, and Hector's a greyhound.

ARMADO: The sweet war-man is dead and rotten. Sweet
　　chucks, beat not the bones of the buried: when he
　　breathed he was a man. But I will forward with my device.

(*To the PRINCESS*) Sweet royalty, bestow on me the sense of hearing.

BEROWNE steps forth

PRINCESS: Speak, brave Hector, we are much delighted.

ARMADO: I do adore thy sweet grace's slipper.

BOYET: Loves her by the foot.

DUMAINE: He may not by the yard.

ARMADO: This Hector far surmounted Hannibal.
    The party is gone.

COSTARD: Fellow Hector, she is gone, she is two months on her way.

ARMADO: What meanest thou?

COSTARD: Faith, unless you play the honest Trojan, the poor wench is cast away. She's quick, the child brags in her belly already, 'tis yours.

ARMADO: Dost thou infamonize me among potentates? Thou shalt die.

COSTARD: Then shall Hector be whipped for Jaquenetta that is quick by him, and hanged for Pompey that is dead by him.

DUMAINE: Most rare Pompey!

BOYET: Renowned Pompey!

BEROWNE: Greater than great, great, great, great Pompey, Pompey the Huge.

DUMAINE: Hector trembles.

BEROWNE: Pompey is moved. More Ates, more Ates, stir them on, stir them on.

DUMAINE: Hector will challenge him.

BEROWNE: Ay, if he have no more man's blood in his belly than will sup a flea.

ARMADO: By the North Pole, I do challenge thee.

COSTARD: I will not fight with a pole, like a northern man. I'll slash, I'll do it by the sword. I bepray you, let me borrow my arms again.

DUMAINE: Room for the incensed Worthies.

COSTARD: I'll do it in my shirt.

DUMAINE: Most resolute Pompey.

MOTH: Master, let me take you a button-hole lower. Do you not see Pompey is uncasing for the combat? What mean you? You will lose your reputation.

ARMADO: Gentlemen and soldiers, pardon me, I will not combat in my shirt.

DUMAINE: You may not deny it, Pompey hath made the challenge.

ARMADO: Sweet bloods, I both may and will.

BEROWNE: What reason have you for't?

ARMADO: The naked truth of it is, I have no shirt. I go woolward for penance.

MOTH: True, and it was enjoined him in Rome for want of linen, since when I'll be sworn he wore none but a dish-clout of Jaquenetta's, and that he wears next his heart, for a favour.

Enter a messenger, MONSIEUR MERCADÉ

MERCADÉ: God save you, madam.

PRINCESS: Welcome Mercadé,
But that thou interrupt'st our merriment.

MERCADÉ: I am sorry, madam, for the news I bring
    Is heavy in my tongue. The King your father –

PRINCESS: Dead, for my life.

MERCADÉ: Even so, my tale is told.

BEROWNE: Worthies away, the scene begins to cloud.

ARMADO: For mine own part, I breathe free breath. I have
    seen the day of wrong through the little hole of
    discretion, and I will right myself like a soldier.

Exeunt the Worthies

KING: How fares your majesty?

QUEEN: Boyet prepare, I will away tonight.

KING: Madam not so, I do beseech you stay.

QUEEN: Prepare I say. I thank you, gracious lords,
    For all your fair endeavours, and entreat,
    Out of a new-sad soul, that you vouchsafe
    In your rich wisdom to excuse or hide
    The liberal opposition of our spirits,
    If overboldly we have borne ourselves
    In the converse of breath, your gentleness
    Was guilty of it. Farewell, worthy lord.
    A heavy heart bears not a nimble tongue.
    Excuse me so, coming too short of thanks,
    For my great suit so easily obtained.

KING: The extreme parts of time extremely forms
    All causes to the purpose of his speed,
    And often at his very loose decides
    That which long process could not arbitrate.
    And though the mourning brow of progeny
    Forbid the smiling courtesy of love
    The holy suit which fain it would convince,
    Yet since love's argument was first on foot,
    Let not the cloud of sorrow jostle it
    From what it purposed, since to wail friends lost

Is not by much so wholesome-profitable
As to rejoice at friends but newly found.

QUEEN: I understand you not, my griefs are double.

BEROWNE: Honest plain words best pierce the ear of grief,
And by these badges understand the King.
For your fair sakes have we neglected time,
Played foul play with our oaths: your beauty, ladies,
Hath much deformed us, fashioning our humours
Even to the opposèd end of our intents,
And what in us hath seemed ridiculous,
As love is full of unbefitting strains,
All wanton as a child, skipping and vain,
Formed by the eye and therefore like the eye,
Full of strange shapes, of habits and of forms,
Varying in subjects as the eye doth roll
To every varied object in his glance;
Which parti-coated presence of loose love
Put on by us, if in your heavenly eyes
Have misbecomed our oaths and gravities,
Those heavenly eyes that look into these faults
Suggested us to make. Therefore ladies,
Our love being yours, the error that love makes
Is likewise yours; we to ourselves prove false
By being once false for ever to be true
To those that make us both, fair ladies, you.
And even that falsehood, in itself a sin,
Thus purifies itself and turns to grace.

QUEEN: We have received your letters full of love,
Your favours the ambassadors of love,
And in our maiden council rated them
At courtship, pleasant jest, and courtesy,
As bombast and as lining to the time;
But more devout than this in our respects
Have we not been, and therefore met your loves
In their own fashion, like a merriment.

DUMAINE: Our letters, madam, showed much more than jest.

LONGAVILLE: So did our looks.

ROSALINE: We did not quote them so.

KING: Now at the latest minute of the hour,
    Grant us your loves.

QUEEN: A time methinks too short
    To make a world-without-end bargain in.
    No no, my lord, your grace is perjured much,
    Full of dear guiltiness, and therefore this:
    If for my love, as there is no such cause,
    You will do aught, this shall you do for me:
    Your oath I will not trust, but go with speed
    To some forlorn and naked hermitage
    Remote from all the pleasures of the world.
    There stay until the twelve celestial signs
    Have brought about the annual reckoning.
    If this austere insociable life
    Change not your offer made in heat of blood;
    If frosts and fasts, hard lodging and thin weeds
    Nip not the gaudy blossoms of your love,
    But that it bear this trial and last love,
    Then at the expiration of the year
    Come challenge me, challenge me by these deserts,
    And by this virgin palm now kissing thine,
    I will be thine; and till that instant shut
    My woeful self up in a mourning house,
    Raining the tears of lamentation
    For the remembrance of my father's death.
    If this thou do deny, let our hands part,
    Neither entitled in the other's heart.

KING: If this, or more than this, I would deny,
    To flatter up these powers of mine with rest
    The sudden hand of death close up mine eye.
    Hence hermit then, my heart is in thy breast.

BEROWNE: And what to me my love, and what to me?

ROSALINE: You must be purgèd too, your sins are rank.
   You are attaint with faults and perjury.

DUMAINE: But what to me my love, but what to me?
   A wife?

KATHERINE: A beard, fair health, and honesty.
   With three-fold love I wish you all these three.

DUMAINE: O shall I say 'I thank you, gentle wife'?

KATHERINE: Not so my lord, a twelvemonth and a day
   I'll mark no words that smooth-faced wooers say.
   Come when the King doth to my lady come;
   Then if I have much love, I'll give you some.

DUMAINE: I'll serve thee true and faithfully till then.

KATHERINE: Yet swear not, lest ye be forsworn again.

LONGAVILLE: What says Maria?

MARIA: At the twelvemonth's end
   I'll change my black gown for a faithful friend.

LONGAVILLE: I'll stay with patience, but the time is long.

MARIA: The liker you, few taller are so young.

BEROWNE: Studies my lady? Mistress, look on me.
   Behold the window of my heart, mine eye,
   What humble suit attends thy answer there.
   Impose some service on me for thy love.

ROSALINE: Oft have I heard of you, my lord Berowne,
   Before I saw you; and the world's large tongue
   Proclaims you for a man replete with mocks,
   Full of comparisons and wounding flouts,
   Which you on all estates will execute
   That lie within the mercy of your wit.
   To weed this wormwood from your fruitful brain,
   And therewithal to win me if you please,
   Without the which I am not to be won,
   You shall this twelvemonth term from day to day

Visit the speechless sick, and still converse
With groaning wretches, and your task shall be
With all the fierce endeavour of your wit,
To enforce the painèd impotent to smile.

BEROWNE: To move wild laughter in the throat of death?
It cannot be, it is impossible.
Mirth cannot move a soul in agony.

ROSALINE: Why that's the way to choke a gibing spirit,
Whose influence is begot of that loose grace
Which shallow laughing hearers give to fools.
A jest's prosperity lies in the ear
Of him that hears it, never in the tongue
Of him that makes it: then if sickly ears,
Deafed with the clamours of their own dear groans,
Will hear your idle scorns, continue then,
And I will have you and that fault withal.
But if they will not, throw away that spirit,
And I shall find you empty of that fault,
Right joyful of your reformation.

BEROWNE: A twelvemonth? Well, befall what will befall,
I'll jest a twelvemonth in an hospital.

QUEEN: Ay sweet my lord, and so I take my leave.

KING: No madam, we will bring you on your way.

BEROWNE: Our wooing doth not end like an old play:
Jack hath not Jill; these ladies' courtesy
Might well have made our sport a comedy.

KING: Come sir, it wants a twelvemonth and a day,
And then 'twill end.

BEROWNE: That's too long for a play.

Enter ARMADO the braggart

ARMADO: Sweet majesty, vouchsafe me.

QUEEN: Was not that Hector?

DUMAINE: The worthy knight of Troy.

ARMADO: I will kiss thy royal finger and take leave. I am a
votary; I have vowed to Jaquenetta to hold the plough for
her sweet love three year. But most esteemed greatness,
will you hear the dialogue that the two learned men have
compiled in praise of the owl and the cuckoo? It should
have followed in the end of our show.

KING: Call them forth quickly, we will do so.

ARMADO: Holla, approach!

*Enter all: HOLOFERNES, NATHANIEL, COSTARD, MOTH,
DULL, JAQUENETTA*

This side is Hiems, winter; this Ver, the spring: the one
maintained by the owl, th' other by the cuckoo. Ver, begin.

SPRING: (*Sings*) When daisies pied and violets blue,
      And lady-smocks all silver-white,
      And cuckoo-buds of yellow hue
      Do paint the meadows with delight,
      The cuckoo then on every tree
      Mocks married men, for thus sings he:
      Cuckoo!
      Cuckoo, cuckoo: O word of fear,
      Unpleasing to a married ear.

      When shepherds pipe on oaten straws,
      And merry larks are ploughmen's clocks,
      When turtles tread, and rooks and daws,
      And maidens bleach their summer smocks,
      The cuckoo then on every tree
      Mocks married men, for thus sings he:
      Cuckoo!
      Cuckoo, cuckoo: O word of fear,
      Unpleasing to a married ear.

WINTER: (*Sings*) When icicles hang by the wall,
      And Dick the shepherd blows his nail,
      And Tom bears logs into the hall,

And milk comes frozen home in pail,
When blood is nipped, and ways be foul,
Then nightly sings the staring owl:
Tu-whit, tu-whoo! a merry note,
While greasy Joan doth keel the pot.

When all aloud the wind doth blow,
And coughing drowns the parson's saw,
And birds sit brooding in the snow,
And Marian's nose looks red and raw,
When roasted crabs hiss in the bowl,
Then nightly sings the staring owl:
Tu-whit, tu-whoo! a merry note,
While greasy Joan doth keel the pot.

ARMADO: The words of Mercury are harsh after the songs of
Apollo. You that way, we this way.

Exeunt